Allies, Adversaries, and International Trade

Allies, Adversaries, and International Trade

Joanne Gowa

PRINCETON UNIVERSITY PRESS

PRINCETON, NEW JERSEY

Library of Congress Cataloging-in-Publication Data
Gowa, Joanne S.
Allies, adversaries, and international trade / Joanne Gowa.
p.   cm.
Includes bibliographical references and index.
ISBN 0-691-03355-2
1. Free trade.   2. Alliances.   3. International trade.   4. East-
West trade (1945–   )   5. World politics—20th century.   I. Title.
HF1713.G57   1993
382—dc20   93-2178

This book has been composed in Linotron Primer

Princeton University Press books are printed on acid-free paper
and meet the guidelines for permanence and durability of the
Committee on Production Guidelines for Book Longevity of the
Council on Library Resources

Printed in the United States of America

1   2   3   4   5   6   7   8   9   10

FOR KATIE, JON, AND TIMMY

Contents

Figures

Tables

Acknowledgments

I WILL ALWAYS BE GRATEFUL to the very large number of people who, in different ways, helped me to write this book.

The gold medal for sheer endurance goes to Robert G. Gilpin, who read the manuscript no less than four times. The silver medal in the same category goes to Robert O. Keohane, who read three drafts. Both made my life miserable each and every time they finished reading. In the end, of course, I am immensely grateful that they did so. Their criticisms were too persuasive to ignore; five is my lucky number; and I think the version that appears in the pages that follow is a distinct improvement over its numerous predecessors.

I am also deeply grateful to colleagues who read the entire manuscript once, all of whom did so with such care that I remain in awe of both their generosity and their insightfulness. They are: Benjamin J. Cohen, Jeffry Frieden, Stephen M. Goldfeld, Avery Goldstein, Peter J. Katzenstein, Peter B. Kenen, David A. Lake, Edward D. Mansfield, Brian M. Pollins, Marc Trachtenberg, Thomas D. Willett, and Beth V. Yarbrough.

Parts of Chapters Two, Three, and Four began life as articles. Along the long road from APSA paper to journal article, numerous people intervened to make the journey even longer. Included among them are many of the scholars already cited, as well as Charles Cameron, Youssef Cohen, John A. C. Conybeare, Henry S. Farber, Stephan Haggard, Richard J. Herring, Arvid Lukauskas, Timothy J. McKeown, George Mailath, John S. Odell, Kenneth A. Oye, Robert Powell, J. David Richardson, and John Gerard Ruggie.

There are also four people who made unconventional and, in at least one case, initially very unwelcome, contributions to this book. For months after I agreed to Peter Katzenstein's request to write an essay for a book he edited, all I wanted was to go back in time and decline to do so. If I had, however, I would not have started to think about the issues this book examines. Thomas Callaghy, who listened very carefully one day as I described the major obstacle that stood between me and the book, made that barrier implode. Without Marc Trachtenberg's help, I would never have found my way around the British archives. Finally and most important was the contribution of Edward Mansfield.

His help was invaluable, not only because he designed and executed the aggregate data analysis that appears in Chapter Four, but also because he never ceased to maintain the kind of interest in the project as a whole that is an extraordinarily rare and precious resource.

Mrs. Edna Lloyd transformed the manuscript into one in which the line spacing, word usage, and other elements of style do not vary randomly throughout the text. She also tracked down the remarkably large number of people scattered across the university who had the best software to execute a particular task. She was an indefatigable source of help. So were three research assistants: Rachel Bronson, Matthias Kaelberer, and Hank Torbert. Walter Lippincott and Malcolm DeBevoise, the director and political science editor of Princeton University Press, respectively, eased the passage of this book through its final stages.

I am also grateful to institutions that provided financial support for the project. Among them are the Center of International Studies at Princeton University and, in particular, its Peter B. Lewis and Boesky Family funds; the Social Science Research Council, which awarded me a MacArthur Foundation Fellowship in International Security; and the Research Foundation of the University of Pennsylvania.

Some of the material in this book has already been published. I am grateful to the *American Political Science Review* for permission to reprint parts of two articles, "Bipolarity, Multipolarity, and Free Trade" (vol. 83, no. 4) and "Power Politics and International Trade" (coauthored with Edward D. Mansfield) (vol. 87, no. 2). I also appreciate the permission of *World Politics* to reprint parts of the article, "Rational Hegemons, Excludable Goods, and Small Groups: An Epitaph for Hegemonic Stability Theory?" (vol. 41, no. 3).

Finally, there are the friends, some of whom are also colleagues, who extended the intangible and priceless help that enabled me to complete this book. Susan Bricklin, Jerry Cohen, Hank Farber, Jeff Frieden, Steve Goldfeld, Judy Goldstein, Pirooz Sholevar, and Herb Walker will always have a very special place in my heart for doing so.

This book is dedicated to my children, Katie, Jon, and Timmy, whom I will love with all my heart forever and ever.

Joanne Gowa
Princeton, New Jersey
February 12, 1993

Allies, Adversaries, and International Trade

Introduction

EVEN A VERY CASUAL INSPECTION of the post–World War II world suggests that the pursuit of power strongly influenced the pursuit of plenty.[1] During the Cold War, international trade closely paralleled the division of the world into two major political-military blocs. Without exception, member states of the North Atlantic Treaty Organization became signatories of the General Agreement on Tariffs and Trade, and members of the Warsaw Treaty Organization joined the Council for Mutual Economic Assistance. In turn, the Coordinating Committee for Multilateral Export Controls (COCOM), essentially a subset of NATO, controlled trade between East and West.[2]

These developments, among others, sparked a heated debate among students of international relations about the impact of power politics on international trade. All those engaged in the debate agreed that the "structure of international trade is determined by the interests and power of states" (Krasner 1976, 317). They disagreed, however, about almost everything else, including, in particular, the role of the Cold War and the utility, if any, of a hegemonic or dominant state.

In explaining the U.S. effort to promote intra-alliance and impede cross-alliance trade, many political scientists and some economists assigned a large role to the Cold War that erupted between the two great powers of the postwar world. That the East-West conflict drove the United States to merge the high politics of security and the low politics of trade is a theme that emerges repeatedly in the work of those scholars who both defined and developed the subfield of international political economy.[3] "From the start of the Cold War," as Benjamin J. Cohen observed,

> official Washington's chief objective was to reconstruct the war-ravaged economies of Western Europe and Japan, and maintain the vigor of the

---

[1] The phrases "pursuit of power" and "pursuit of plenty" derive, of course, from Viner (1948).

[2] COCOM includes all of NATO's members except Iceland. It also includes Japan and Australia.

[3] See, for example, Cohen (1974); Gilpin (1975, 1981); Keohane and Nye (1970, 1977); Katzenstein (1978); Krasner (1976); and Ruggie (1972).

undamaged Canadian economy, so that these countries could all serve as effective barriers to communist expansion. Toward this end the United States . . . promoted through GATT a broad program of worldwide liberalization of industrial trade that frequently benefited its allies directly at its own expense. ([1974] 1991, 102)

Others interpreting the genesis of the postwar economic order, however, gave only a bit part, if any, to the Cold War. Instead, they assigned the leading role to the emergence of the United States as a benevolent world despot. In advancing what would later become known as hegemonic stability theory, Charles P. Kindleberger argued that, because international free trade is a public good, it has a political prerequisite: the existence of a hegemonic power (1973).[4] In the late nineteenth and early twentieth centuries, Britain, according to Kindleberger, supplied the public goods essential to global economic stability; in the post–World War II period, the United States did so. Moreover, Kindleberger claimed, it was not the Cold War but the chaos of the interwar period that prompted the United States to act.

Although its assumptions about public goods and rational hegemons, among others, have become highly controversial, the appeal of hegemonic theory inheres in the clarity and rigor of the argument that supports it.[5] Its intuitive appeal, however, is much more limited. Publicly-minded despots are aliens in the world that is the conventional referent of most students of international relations.[6] Among the latter, the dominant belief is that the play of great-power politics determines whether open international markets will exist. As Robert G. Gilpin argues,

[4] The hegemonic stability label is frequently applied as well to the arguments of both Robert G. Gilpin and Stephen D. Krasner. Kindleberger emphasizes the stability of the international system, however, while Gilpin and Krasner focus on the self-interest of the dominant state (Gilpin 1975, 1981; Krasner 1976).

It should be noted that Kindleberger himself prefers the term *leader* to *hegemon* because of the "overtones of force, threat [and] pressure" associated with the latter (1986, 841).

[5] The rigor of hegemonic theory owes as much to subsequent contributors to the debate that emerged about it as it does to Kindleberger. Some important contributors are Conybeare (1984); Keohane (1984); Snidal (1985b); and Yarbrough and Yarbrough (1992). As Chapter Two makes clear, this does not imply that these individuals endorse hegemonic theory.

[6] In most analyses that followed Kindleberger's, the claim was that hegemons supplied public goods as an inadvertent by-product of their pursuit of private interests. Thus, hegemons were seen as somewhat absentminded, benevolent despots. See, for example, Snidal (1985b) for an incisive discussion of the varied interests and methods that different hegemons might pursue.

the modern world economy has evolved through the emergence of great national economies that have successively become dominant.... An economic system ... does not arise spontaneously owing to the operation of an invisible hand and in the absence of the exercise of power. Rather, every economic system rests on a particular political order; its nature cannot be understood apart from politics. (1975, 40–1)

Explanations based on the Cold War specifically and on great-power interactions more generally are appealing because they capture an essential dimension of politics that hegemonic theory does not. Their analytic foundations are much weaker, however. Those who argue that the post-1945 free-trade system was an "integral part of high politics and alliance solidarity" tend to assume rather than to explain the relationship between power politics and interstate trade (Haggard and Simmons 1987, 503). Yet, a perfectly plausible case can be made that alliance cohesion and free trade are, in fact, inversely related. As Kenneth N. Waltz argues,

many seem to believe that a growing closeness of [economic] interdependence improves the chances of peace. But close interdependence means closeness of contact and raises the prospect of occasional conflict. The fiercest civil wars and the bloodiest international ones are fought within arenas populated by highly similar people whose affairs are closely knit. (1979, 138)[7]

In addition, students of international relations who emphasize the role of the Cold War implicitly assume that the post–World War II linkage between political-military alliances and free trade is sui generis. The logic that supports this assumption is not self-evident, however. Based on the extant literature, the inference that the Cold War is simply one among many cases is as plausible as is the inference that it is unique.

In this book, I develop what I hope is an intuitively appealing *and* analytically rigorous explanation of the impact of power politics on inter-state trade. In order to do so, I construct a very simple game-theoretic model to address the question of substantive importance. That question is whether free trade is more likely within than across alliances. More precisely, I address this question: Under what, if any,

[7] It is also possible that these two variables are not related at all. This will be the case if, for example, alliance members confront perfectly elastic import supply and export demand curves. Chapters Three and Four discuss these alternatives in detail.

conditions does it make sense for states to trade more freely with their allies than with their adversaries?

THE ARGUMENT IN BRIEF

Beginning in Chapter Three, I analyze the impact of the anarchic structure of international politics on the exchange of goods and services among states. Prior to doing so, I argue that hegemonic stability theory, the preeminent system-level theory of the relationship between power politics and free trade, does not resolve the question of the political correlates of open international markets. The principal objective of Chapter Two is to make explicit the foundations of this claim about hegemonic theory.

Here, I summarize the core argument of this book. I contend that the play of power politics is an inexorable element of any agreement to open international markets, because of the security externalities that trade produces.[8] These externalities arise because the source of gains from trade is the increased efficiency with which domestic resources can be employed. As a consequence, trade frees economic resources for military uses. Thus, trade enhances the potential military power of any country that engages in it.

The anarchic structure of the international system, in turn, compels its constituent states to attend closely to the military power and potential of both prospective and actual allies and adversaries. It does so because the absence of any supranational authority in the international system enables a state either to threaten or to actually resort to force at any time to achieve its goals. The probability that a state will do so depends in part upon its power. The latter, in turn, depends partly upon its real income.

As a consequence, the real-income gains that motivate free trade are also the source of the security externalities that can either impede or facilitate trade: Trade with an adversary produces a security diseconomy; trade with an ally produces a positive externality. In either case, agreements to open international markets create a divergence between the private and social costs of trade.[9] A socially suboptimal level of trade

---

[8] Externalities are uncompensated costs or benefits that an agent inflicts or confers on third parties (Yeager and Tureck 1983–84, 660).

[9] This is so because the optimization rule for individual agents is to equate marginal costs and private marginal benefits. The optimization rule for society as a whole, however,

results. As a result, government intervention in trade can be welfare-enhancing for the nation as a whole.

In other words, because trade generates security externalities, adherence to a policy of free and non-discriminatory trade may not be optimal for states in an anarchic international system. In Chapter Three, I consider these external effects explicitly. Doing so leads me to two conclusions: (1) free trade is more likely within than across political-military alliances; and (2) the evolutionary prospects of alliances vary: Those that are the products of bipolar systems are more likely to evolve into free-trade coalitions than are their multipolar counterparts.

Thus, the argument I advance in this book suggests that the Cold War experience was neither unique nor irrational. The post–1945 pattern was not simply a consequence of the ideological divide that existed between the United States and the Soviet Union. The external effects associated with trade imply that nations *should* attempt to induce trade to follow the flag. This prescription applies not only after but also before 1945. Nevertheless, it does not apply to all states at all times. Attempts to use the exchange of goods and services to influence the play of great-power politics can succeed only if a state can affect its terms of trade. Thus, as the literature on economic statecraft more generally suggests, a rational state will attempt to bind trade to the flag only if it has some monopoly or monopsony power in world markets.[10] The role of market power is explained in detail in Chapter Three.

Level of Analysis

As is undoubtedly already obvious, the focus of this book is on the impact of the structure of international politics on patterns of interstate trade. Others students of international relations, however, assume that these patterns are the products of politics *within* rather than across national borders.[11] In terms that have become conventional in the field, this book takes a system-level, or "Third Image," approach to interna-

---

requires that marginal costs equal marginal *social* returns. For further discussion, see Boadway and Wildasin (1984).

[10] See D. Baldwin (1985) for a wide-ranging discussion of the varied types and uses of what he labels "economic statecraft."

[11] For examples of literature in this tradition, see Frieden (1988); Gourevitch (1986); Hillman (1989); Katzenstein (1978); Lavergne (1983); Lohmann and O'Halloran (1991); Magee, Brock, and Young (1989); Pincus (1977); Ray (1981); and Rogowski (1989).

tional relations rather than a domestic political, or "Second Image," approach. Thus, it treats states as unitary actors.

In Second-Image models, the distributional consequences of free trade explain deviations from Pareto-optimality.[12] That is, a nation might adopt protection despite its adverse aggregate welfare consequences if free trade inflicts losses on some groups *and* a disproportionate amount of political power accrues to those groups.[13] Under these circumstances, economic efficiency is unlikely to be the only metric used to set national trade policy.

There is no question but that the play of domestic politics influences decisions about trade policy. Also indisputable, however, is that strategic interaction between political officials and special interest groups does not wholly determine these decisions.[14] In large countries, for example, Pareto-optimality may dictate the imposition of tariffs. Especially in the case of great powers, therefore, a system-level analysis seems to promise to increase our understanding of the political determinants of interstate trade.

More generally, whether the assumption of a rational or unitary actor is "useful or trivializes the analysis of international interactions," as Bruce Bueno de Mesquita and David Lalman observe, is "ultimately, an empirical question." If this assumption facilitates the process of understanding patterns of behavior, they note, it will be helpful, and it will "not excessively simplify and trivialize what is undoubtedly a very complex process" (1992, 27). As the discussion immediately below shows, empirical tests of the system-level theory advanced in this book do indeed yield results that help to explain patterns of trade between nations over time.

THE EMPIRICAL EVIDENCE IN BRIEF

Because political-military alliances internalize the external effects associated with trade, nations should, all else being equal, trade more

[12] This brief discussion is not meant to imply that there is only one approach to an explanation of protection based on domestic politics. Differences exist not only among formal models but also among the implicit models that are the basis of empirical studies of tariff formation in different countries. For a good review, see Nelson (1988).

[13] See Chapter Two for an explanation of the welfare effects of tariffs.

[14] For a review of the relevant theoretical and empirical literature, see R. Baldwin (1985) and Lavergne (1983).

freely within than across alliances. A rigorous empirical test of this proposition does not, at first glance, appear to present any insuperable obstacles. No intractable problems seem to confront either the development or the implementation of a research design intended to determine whether trade barriers between allies are lower than those between adversaries.

As the discussion in Chapter Four makes clear, construction of an appropriate research design *is* easy. For various reasons detailed in that chapter, however, its execution is not easy. Thus, I emphasize here that the results of the empirical analyses presented in this book need to be interpreted cautiously. The implicit or explicit caveat emptor that applies to almost all empirical research in the social sciences also applies here.

That being said, Chapter Four presents a statistical analysis of the relationship between alliances and trade. Using data drawn from an eighty-year period that begins in 1905, the chapter evaluates the impact of alliances on the trade flows of seven countries: the United States, the Soviet Union, Great Britain, France, Italy, Germany, and Japan.[15] The analysis controls for various economic determinants of trade, including gross national product, population, and distance. The control variables, the composition of the sample, and the choice and measures of independent and dependent variables are discussed in detail in Chapter Four. Of primary concern here, then, is a brief summary of the results of the statistical analysis.

The results support the argument. Between 1905 and 1985, alliances have had a direct, statistically significant, and large effect upon bilateral trade. Moreover, analysis of the aggregate data demonstrates unambiguously that, on average, alliances have had a much stronger effect on trade in a bipolar than in a multipolar world. Also made clear is that these results do not depend on whether the trading partners are democratic, members of preferential trading arrangements, or parties to military disputes.

Thus, the results of the aggregate-data analysis reported in Chapter Four confirm the hypotheses that emerge from the simple game-theoretic model that I construct and analyze in Chapter Three. Free trade is more likely within than across alliances, and alliances are more likely to evolve into free-trade coalitions if they are embedded within bipolar than within multipolar systems. The results also demonstrate,

[15] At a small price in terms of accuracy, Germany (rather than West Germany) and the Soviet Union (rather than Russia) are used throughout the text in order to simplify the presentation.

however, that there is substantial variation across alliances with respect to their impact on trade that cannot be attributed exclusively to systemic polarity.

In an attempt to elucidate other sources of cross-alliance variation, I present a case study of the impact of alliance entry on trade policy. In Chapter Five, I analyze whether the conclusion of the Anglo-French Entente, in 1904, affected British trade policy. The principal reason I chose to examine this Entente is that it appears to be a deviant case. According to the results of the aggregate data analysis presented in Chapter Four, alliances did *not* influence trade flows before World War I. Although these findings do not, of course, necessarily apply to all alliances that existed in the pre-1914 decade, the case study makes it crystal clear that the results reported in Chapter Four apply not only to alliances in general but also to the Anglo-French case in particular. As such, the case study allows me to speculate about why the pre-1914 period deviated from the norm. It also serves as a springboard to the more abstract discussion of cross-alliance variation that is the focus of Chapter Six.

In Chapter Six, I examine several factors, both political and economic, that might explain this variation. Among them are differences across alliances in the magnitude of social returns to trade; in relative factor endowments; and in market power. A discussion of these factors yields insights into two issues that have long puzzled students of international political economy. The first is the stark contrast between the impact of great-power politics on trade before 1914 and after 1945. The second is the failure of high levels of interstate trade to deter the outbreak of World War I. I discuss both issues in the latter half of Chapter Six.

In Chapter Seven, I reprise the argument and evidence presented in this book. In that chapter, I also note that the findings in this book imply that the conventional division of international relations into two discrete subfields (i.e., international security and international political economy) makes little sense.

The first task of this book, however, is to establish that a serious flaw exists in hegemonic stability theory, the analytically most rigorous Third-Image explanation of the political correlates of economic order. In Chapter Two, therefore, I review debates about hegemonic theory. I do so in order to make clear that the theory does not provide a compelling explanation of the political determinants of interstate trade in an anarchic world.

Hegemonic Stability Theory: A Critical Review

THE MERE MENTION of hegemonic stability theory now tends to evoke a chorus of groans even from those who initially found it compelling. The decibel level rises as the set expands to include others who have been its most incisive critics. Because no other system-level theory has yet supplanted it, however, hegemonic stability theory continues to occupy a preeminent position in the existing literature.

Critics of hegemonic theory argue that it is based upon indefensible assumptions about rational hegemons, excludable goods, and small groups. In this chapter, I contend that these criticisms are not fatal to the theory. Nevertheless, I concur in the overall judgment rendered by critics of the theory. Hegemonic theory *ought* to be displaced from its position of prominence, for a simple reason: It neglects the essence of the domain to which it applies, that is, the politics of trade in an anarchic world. As such, it cannot possibly explain the relationship between the play of great-power politics and interstate trade. A theory that can do so should, therefore, supplant it.

HEGEMONIC STABILITY THEORY

The apparent erosion of the postwar international economic order that began in the early 1970s led to a surge of interest among scholars about the political correlates of open international markets. That surge produced what appeared at the time to be a compelling argument: The world was safe from tariff wars and great depressions if and only if a dominant state or hegemonic power existed.

Developing what Robert O. Keohane several years later would label "hegemonic stability" theory, Kindleberger argued in 1973 that international free trade was a public good (Kindleberger 1973; Keohane 1980, 132). As such, Kindleberger maintained, its reliable supply depended on the existence of a hegemonic state. As Kindleberger put it, "for the world economy to be stabilized, there has to be a stabilizer, one stabilizer" (1973, 305).

11

Column

	Cooperate	Defect
Cooperate	*R,R*	*S,T*
Defect	*T,S*	*P,P*

Row

FIGURE 2.1. The Prisoners' Dilemma Game
Note: T > R > P > S; R ⩾ (T + S)/2

Thus, the properties and problems of public goods provide the analytic basis of hegemonic theory. Unlike private goods (like Big Macs or chocolate chip cookies), public goods (like nuclear deterrence or clean air) are nonrival in consumption and nonexcludable: that is, any individual's consumption of these goods does not preclude their consumption by others; and no one can be excluded or prevented from consuming such goods whether or not he has paid for them. As a result, rational actors have an incentive to free ride rather than to assume any of the cost of the good's supply.

The problem that inheres in the supply of public goods, therefore, can be represented as a Prisoners' Dilemma game. The rank ordering of preferences of those engaged in any PD game is: $T > R > P > S$. These payoffs represent, respectively, the payoff to unilateral defection (i.e., the "temptation" to defect); the payoff to mutual cooperation; the payoff to mutual defection; and the payoff to unilateral cooperation (i.e., the "sucker's" payoff). The corresponding payoff matrix, which any student of international relations can now produce in his or her sleep, is shown in figure 2.1.

Given these payoffs, defection is a dominant strategy for each player (i.e., each is better off defecting than cooperating regardless of what the other does): $T > R$ and $P > S$. As a result, each player refuses (defects) rather than contributes (cooperates) to the supply of the public good. A Pareto-inferior equilibrium outcome (P,P), results: No one contributes; no public good is produced;[1] and both would be better off if they had cooperated to supply the public good.[2]

[1] A Pareto-superior equilibrium is one in which at least one individual would be better off and no individual would be worse off than at the existing outcome.

[2] As discussed in detail in Chapter Three, this is necessarily the case only if the game is played a finite number of times and if complete information obtains.

If states locked into an international free-trade PD are to escape their dilemma, Kindleberger argued, a hegemon must exist. Because of its relative size in the international system, Kindleberger argues, a hegemon "has an incentive to see that the collective good is provided, even if he has to bear the full burden of providing it himself" (Olson 1971, 50).

Distinctly casual empiricism seems to support Kindleberger's argument. British hegemony in the nineteenth and early twentieth centuries and U.S. hegemony in the midtwentieth century coincided with relatively open international markets. The inability of the British and the unwillingness of the United States to lead coincided with the construction of "beggar-thy-neighbor" trading blocs in the interwar period. The apparent decline in U.S. hegemony in recent decades, and the simultaneous increase in trade barriers among the industrialized countries, also appear to support Kindleberger's claim. Whether the apparent correlation between hegemony and free trade actually exists or, even if it does, whether it represents a causal relationship has, of course, become extremely controversial.[3]

Of particular concern to this chapter, however, is not the empirical validity, but the analytic integrity of hegemonic theory. Critics have challenged three assumptions fundamental to the theory. They argue that: (1) rational hegemons, according to standard international trade theory, adopt an optimal tariff rather than free trade; (2) the provision of open international markets implies the supply of excludable rather than public goods; and (3) small groups are close substitutes for hegemons. Thus, they conclude, hegemony is not necessary for—and, indeed, may be antithetical to—a stable world economy based on market exchange.

These are potentially powerful criticisms. If persuasive, they would destroy the analytic foundations of a theory already the target of attack on empirical grounds (Conybeare 1983; McKeown 1982, 1983). In succeeding sections of this chapter, I assess these arguments and conclude that each argument has considerable validity but that none is as damaging to the theory as is claimed. This is so because, on economic grounds alone, a nonmyopic, rational hegemon may reject an optimal tariff; exclusion from a free-trade accord is itself a public good; and hegemons enjoy a clear advantage relative to small groups with respect

[3] For examples of the extensive literature that both vehemently and sometimes persuasively object to each and every historical interpretation in this paragraph, see McKeown (1982, 1983); Oye (1985b); and Russett (1985).

to the supply of international public goods.[4] Strategic interdependence, incomplete information, and barriers to small or "k" group formation are the core elements of the argument I present here.

The arguments of its most incisive critics, in short, do not demolish hegemonic stability theory. Nevertheless, the theory does have a fatal weakness: It fails to acknowledge the influence of power politics on the architecture of the world trading order.

In the last section of this chapter, I make clear the markedly apolitical character of the theory in order to establish the raison d'être of this book: to construct an explanation of inter-state trade that confronts directly rather than denies implicitly the political foundations of trade in an anarchic world.

RATIONAL HEGEMONS AND FREE TRADE

In a wide-ranging and perceptive review of the political economy of international trade published in 1984, John A. C. Conybeare makes an important (and, albeit only in retrospect, wholly obvious) point about hegemonic stability theory. The attribution to a hegemon of free-trade preferences, he observes, does not make any sense.

According to standard international trade theory, in the presence of perfectly competitive markets, free trade maximizes the real income of a *small* country (i.e., any country that does not have sufficient market power to influence its terms of trade, defined as the relative price of its exports on world markets). Figure 2.2, a staple of elementary textbooks in trade, demonstrates why free trade is welfare-maximizing for these countries. The figure depicts domestic demand and supply for a good that is also available on world markets at a price, P_w. Domestic producers supply Q_0 of the good; consumers demand Q_3. The difference between the two is the amount imported (i.e., $Q_3 - Q_0$). A tariff increases the domestic price of the imported good from P_w to $P_w(1 + t)$. As a result, it increases domestic output to Q_1, reduces consumption to Q_2, and decreases imports to $Q_2 - Q_1$.

[4] Some theorists acknowledge that small groups are imperfect substitutes for hegemons (for example, Keohane 1984); others do not. Snidal argues, for example, that the "conflict between individual and collective interests does not guarantee the failure of cooperation in the absence of hegemony. Collective action is possible, even likely, and may result both in higher levels of cooperation and in a preferable distribution of the costs and benefits of cooperation" (1985b, 598).

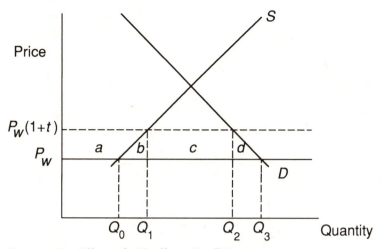

FIGURE 2.2. Effects of a Tariff in a Small Country

This creates a gain in producer surplus equal to area a; a gain in government revenue equal to area c; and a loss of consumer surplus equal to $a + b + c + d$. The result is a deadweight loss of areas $b + d$. Thus, when a small country imposes a tariff, it incurs a net welfare loss. Because producers gain less than consumers lose, the latter could compensate the former and still be better off than if a tariff were imposed.

The story that applies to *large* countries is different, however. Standard international trade theory makes clear that free trade will *not* maximize the income of any state large enough to influence its terms of trade. Instead, an optimal tariff will do so—that is, a tax on trade set at the point that maximizes the net gain that accrues from the resulting improved terms and reduced volume of trade.

The logic that supports the optimal-tariff argument is straightforward. An optimal tariff has the same effects as does any other tariff. It also has one other important effect, however. When a country can influence its terms of trade, it can reduce the relative price of its imports. Thus, even though an optimal tariff still inflicts the same production and consumption costs associated with the use of any tariff, its terms-of-trade effect makes its net impact welfare-increasing. Figure 2.3 illustrates this point.

As in figure 2.2, figure 2.3 shows the domestic market for a good that can be imported at its world price, P_w. Domestic production is Q_0; domestic consumption is Q_3. The difference between them is the amount

15

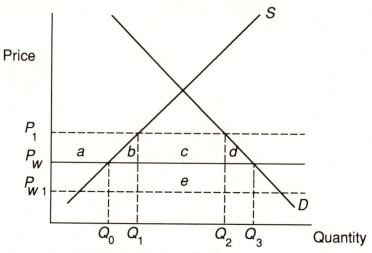

FIGURE 2.3. Effects of an Optimal Tariff

imported (i.e., $Q_3 - Q_0$). Unlike the small-country case that figure 2.2 depicts, however, the use of a tariff by a large country will reduce the world price of its imports. Thus, the post-tariff world price of the good is P_{w1}. The post-tariff domestic price is shown as P_1.[5]

As a result, the use of an optimal tariff enables a large country to increase the amount of tariff revenue that accrues by an area equal to that of e in figure 2.3. Because the tariff can always be set such that $e > b + d$, if a country can influence its terms of trade, a tariff will always increase its welfare.[6] Thus, some observers conclude, only an irrational hegemon would conform to the behavioral prescriptions of hegemonic theory.[7]

It is clear, therefore, that some qualifications are essential in order to make the attribution of free-trade preferences to a hegemon sensible. Among the possibilities is the ability of a hegemon to use more efficient means than its influence over its terms of trade to redistribute income

[5] Because of its terms-of-trade effect, the tariff has to be larger than that used in the standard case if the objective is to raise domestic prices to the same level as in that case.

[6] I interpret the existence of a hegemon as implying that no other state possesses market power. If this were not the case, the arguments about retaliation detailed in the next chapter would apply. Although this may appear to be a strong assumption, it seems consistent with the definition of, and connotations associated with, the term *hegemon*.

[7] This claim is intended to apply only to singleminded hegemons. Those that pursue political as well as economic goals, critics acknowledge, may prefer free trade for political reasons. See, for example, Conybeare (1984).

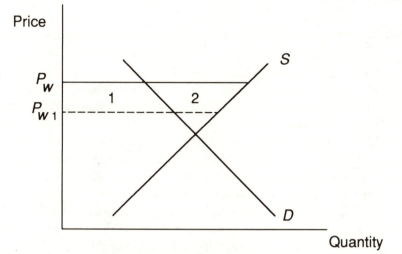

FIGURE 2.4.   Cost to the Exporting Country
Source: Wonnacott 1987, 54.

from its trading partners to itself. A more important—and, perhaps, more practical—qualification inheres in the logic of limit-pricing models, which suggests that strategic considerations may deter the use of an optimal tariff by a hegemon.

The possession of power, in the trade-theory sense, for example, necessarily implies the use of a tariff only if the hegemon cannot find a more efficient method of global income redistribution. As figure 2.4 demonstrates, a tariff is an inefficient instrument of income redistribution. A tariff that lowers world prices from P_w to P_{w1} leads to a loss of producer surplus of areas 1 and 2 and a gain to consumers of area 1. Thus, other states lose more than the hegemon gains (Caves and Jones, 1973, 244). Therefore, in its *own* long-run interest in enhancing its revenue base, the dominant state has an incentive to pursue either of two potentially Pareto-superior alternatives to trade barriers: bribery or taxation.[8]

In practice, the transaction costs associated with both alternatives are likely to exceed the deadweight loss produced by a tariff. In the case of small states engaged in a collective effort to bribe the hegemon to adopt free trade, a public-good problem arises: Each small state that is potentially party to such bribery has an incentive to let others assume

[8] For a brief discussion of bribery as an alternative to tariff retaliation in the context of two states of equal size, see Conybeare (1984, 14–15).

its costs. Free-riding can be prevented only in the unlikely event that either the hegemon or an agent of the small states can cheaply discriminate among the exports of a large number of small countries.

Designing, implementing, and enforcing a system to tax other states is likely to be prohibitively costly to the hegemon. Although the international equivalent of a lump-sum tax might leave small states better off than would an optimal tariff, these states may recognize that they would be even better off as free riders: The hegemon's threat to sanction tax evaders may not be credible to them. The hegemon's situation is analogous to that of the incumbent firm in the chain-store paradox: The firm confronts a trade-off between the short-term costs to it of punishing defiance and the longer term costs to its reputation if it does not do so.[9] In any case, unilateral imposition of an optimal tariff is likely to be less costly to the hegemon than the theoretically Pareto-superior alternative of taxation.

Despite the dearth of alternative means of redistributing income in its favor, a clear-thinking, nonmyopic hegemon may still reject the optimal tariff recommended to it by standard trade theory. Its interest in doing so would be to preserve its monopoly power, that is, to deter the formation of trading blocs that would eliminate its privileged position as the only country capable of influencing its terms of trade. Thus, a rational hegemon would act on the same logic that can motivate a domestic monopolist to set the price of its product below its short-run maximizing level. The incumbent firm thereby attempts to deter entry into its markets. By "limit-pricing" (i.e., pricing to limit entry), the monopolist seeks to signal potential entrants that it is a low-cost producer (Milgrom and Roberts 1982). The monopolist's ability to sacrifice short-run gains to earn higher long-run returns depends on the existence of both costs to entry and asymmetric information about its costs of production.[10]

A rational, nonmyopic hegemon may set its tariff at less than the short-run optimal level under analogous conditions—if, for example, it has some private information about the elasticity of global demand and

[9] For a formal analysis of the chain-store paradox, see Kreps and Wilson (1982, 253–79).

[10] Since a potential entrant is aware of the incentives of an established firm to engage in limit pricing, the incumbent's strategy may not work. In addition, under some conditions, it will not be possible for a low-cost producer to use price as a strategic variable to distinguish itself from a high-cost producer (that is, a pooling, rather than a separating equilibrium, may occur). See Milgrom and Roberts (1982, 443–59).

supply curves and if small countries organizing to exert countervailing power in world markets were to incur some costs in doing so.[11] That a hegemon might indeed have private information about global markets follows logically from its incentives to become informed about them. A small country, in contrast, has little incentive to acquire such information, because it cannot influence its terms of trade. That significant transaction costs are incurred in the process of forming customs unions follows from the distributional effects both within and across its potential members that the setting of uniform external trade barriers evokes (McMillan 1986, 67).

The trading practices of both Britain and the United States suggest that the analogy to limit pricing may be of more than just analytic interest. Midnineteenth-century Britain, according to one observer, maintained its tariffs at less than optimal levels in order to fix its "monopoly of manufactures on the rest of the world for a few more decades than its natural term" (Cunningham, cited in McCloskey 1980, 304).[12] The logic of limit-pricing apparently impressed itself on the United States only after it imposed the Smoot-Hawley tariff in 1930. The latter provoked the construction of trading blocs abroad, inducing U.S. attempts to lower trade barriers not long thereafter.[13]

In short, because an attempt to exploit its power in the short run may undermine that power over time, a nonmyopic, rational hegemon might reject an optimal tariff. Although the limit-pricing argument does not support an inference that free trade—the international analogue of

[11] In his more recent work, Conybeare notes that heavy export taxes may induce substitution which, in turn, dictates the use of lighter taxes in the interest of maximizing long-run profits. Conybeare dismisses this argument unpersuasively: He claims that "long-term elasticity . . . arguments merely assert that the hegemon is not really a hegemon" (1987, 72).

[12] Donald McCloskey has argued that Britain lost "at most" 4 percent of national income when it chose free trade rather than an optimal tariff (1980, 305). McCloskey's analysis relies on "intuition," notes Bhagwati, who observes that Douglas Irwin has

estimated British foreign trade elasticities for that period and calculated the welfare loss of unilateral tariff reduction at about 0.5 percent of national income in the very short run. As Irwin points out, though, longer-run elasticities imply an extremely small welfare loss, and if foreign tariff reductions are factored in (resulting from Britain's demonstration effect promoting free trade) Irwin finds that Britain was made better off. (cited in Bhagwati 1988, 29–30)

[13] For an analysis that suggests that the Great Depression would have led to the same outcome even without the U.S. provocation, see Eichengreen, cited in Bhagwati (1988, 22).

competitive prices at the domestic level—will prevail, it does suggest that self-imposed restraints on the use of an optimal tariff can be in the strictly economic self-interest of a farsighted, clear-thinking hegemon.

In addition, because the limit-pricing analogue suggests that it may be cheaper to forgo an optimal tariff than standard trade theory implies, it also suggests that the incidence of decisions to do so for political reasons may be higher than would otherwise be expected. Thus, for example, the introduction of long-term elasticities into empirical estimates of the welfare losses incurred by Britain as a consequence of its unilateral adoption of free trade in the midnineteenth century suggests that the magnitude of these losses was "extremely small."[14] Although Britain's repeal of the Corn Laws is conventionally attributed to domestic politics, the British case nevertheless suggests that a hegemon does not need very strong political incentives to adopt free trade; the economic losses it incurs by doing so can be insignificant.

In sum, even the exclusively economic self-interest of a rational hegemon may not persuade it to adopt the optimal tariff of standard trade theory. Its preferences will depend on the relative costs of bribery, taxation, and tariffs, and on its ability to deter entry via the strategic use of its market power. It is certainly possible that, under some circumstances, a hegemon will choose an optimal tariff as conventionally defined. Under other circumstances, however—even in situations in which political factors do not influence its choice—it may not do so.

Free Trade and Public Goods

The public-good premise of hegemonic theory has become controversial. Free trade, some critics contend, *is* excludable. "Common markets as well as discriminatory tariffs and nontariff barriers against particular countries, particular goods, and even particular goods from particular countries," Duncan Snidal argues, for example, "indicate the possibilities for extensive and fine-tuned control over exclusion" (1985b, 595). Conybeare makes a similar argument: "Countries may, individually or collectively, penalize a country that attempts to impose a nationally advantageous tariff at the expense of the international community" (1984, 6). Thus, some observers contend, free trade is not a public good because it fails to fulfill the nonexcludability attribute of such goods.

[14] See note 12 above.

In principle, this claim is correct, which suggests that some qualification of hegemonic theory is again in order. But implicit in the argument about exclusion is an assumption that each state benefits from sanctioning would-be free riders. If, however, the policing of a cooperative agreement is costly, enforcement itself becomes a public good (Axelrod and Keohane 1985, 226–54). As Michael Laver observes, costly exclusion "simply replaces one collective action problem with another, the problem of raising exclusion costs" (1980, 200).

Whenever defection is either ambiguous or easily concealed, sanctioning is likely to be costly (Oye 1985a, 15). Ambiguity threatens to make punishment appear as provocation, provoking a feud which will not eliminate the alleged offense but which will impose costs on the would-be enforcer. Yet ambiguity is virtually indigenous to PDs, because incentives to conceal cheating are strong. As George J. Stigler observes of industrial cartels, for example, "the detection of secret price-cheating will, of course, be as difficult as interested people can make it" (1964, 47).

Informational asymmetries pervade trade agreements, arising from the varied sources of ambiguity inherent in them. Among these sources are the need to translate international agreements into domestic law; difficulty in determining whether conditions of breach exist; inability to specify illegal behavior precisely; and the possibility of currency manipulation as a substitute for overt action on trade (Yarbrough and Yarbrough 1987, 7–9). In addition, would-be free riders may conceal cheating by shipping their exports through third countries.

Thus, as is true of many Prisoners' Dilemma games, monitoring, assessing, and punishing attempts to cheat are crucial but costly aspects of international trade agreements. As a result, it becomes individually rational but collectively suboptimal for states to free-ride on the enforcement efforts of others: Whenever incomplete information exists, exclusion of deviants from a trade agreement itself becomes a public good.[15]

In short, although technically excludable, free trade nonetheless presents public-good problems under realistic assumptions about the costs of sanctions. Even if the public-good problems that may inhere in other regimes ancillary to the trade regime are set aside, open international markets do involve the supply of a public good.

[15] Thus, the supply of information assumes a central role in recent analyses of international regimes. See, for example, Keohane (1984, 259); Russett (1985, 222).

Small Groups as Substitutes

Small-group critics of hegemonic theory contend that even large-number systems can successfully resolve collective action problems if there exists a "k," or subgroup, of actors who would profit by doing so even if only its members absorb the costs involved. Again, this criticism is well-founded. There is no basis in public-good theory for the assumption that the existence of a hegemon is essential to a global free-trade system. As Keohane observes, the "theory of collective goods does not properly imply that cooperation among a few countries should be impossible. . . . Logically, hegemony should not be a necessary condition for the emergence of cooperation in an oligopolistic system" (1984, 38).

Small-group theory, however, addresses but does not resolve two issues critical to the ability of a group of states to substitute for a hegemon: the group's origins and its enforcement mechanisms. Although game-theoretic solutions to generic problems of both kinds do exist, it is not clear how useful they are in the context of the case at hand. It *is* clear, however, that their utility varies not only across the constituent states of any given international system but also across different international systems.

Origins

Analyses of small groups attribute their origin in part to exogenous factors. Prominent among the latter is the legacy of hegemony. Snidal, for example, notes that

> collective action will [not] always result when the possibility for joint gains is present. Collective action will depend on a host of relevant circumstances (e.g., . . . existence of relevant regime rules or conventions). It will also be affected by many of the same factors associated with the relative rise and decline of states. These exogenous factors may be inherently conflictual (e.g., the last-gasp imperialist rivalries leading up to World War I) or mutually beneficial and conducive to cooperation (e.g., the system-wide growth that led to the "decline" of the United States relative to other advanced capitalist countries in the last two decades). (1985b, 594–5; cf. Haggard and Simmons 1987, 506)

In some respects, the relatively casual treatment of the issue of "k" group genesis is unimpeachable. First, proponents of small-group theory themselves readily acknowledge that they do not systematically address the issue.[16] Second, hegemonic theory does only slightly better on this score. Its implicit assumption is that a hegemon emerges as a consequence of a system-wide war. Finally, no theory of international cooperation should be indicted simply because it cannot explain the entire life cycle of interstate cooperation.

Yet the failure to address the issue systematically is troubling, for several reasons. The legacy of hegemony can explain the rise of small groups only if the international system evolves peacefully from a hegemonic to a nonhegemonic structure. Yet such power transitions can be potent sources of war (Gilpin 1981; Organski and Kugler 1980). Its relative neglect of the genesis issue also leaves small-group theory mute before a problem central to the field of international political economy. Given that the great powers are always few in number, the theory is unable to explain why there are wide variations in the capacity of different systems to support market exchange among their constituent states.[17]

The relative inattention to small-group origins also relies implicitly upon a deus ex machina to dismantle a formidable barrier to entry that a small group would otherwise confront: The need to agree on the cooperative equilibrium it will thereafter enforce. The literature on strategic interaction among firms in imperfectly competitive markets has been strongly criticized for its silence on this aspect of collusion (see, e.g., Shapiro 1989). This criticism applies a fortiori to discussions of free-trade "k" groups. If neither oligopolies nor would-be international "k" groups can reach agreement on what is to be enforced, it is, as James Friedman observes in the industrial context, "cold comfort to know that the firms, should they ever find themselves at the equilibrium, would never seek to deviate from it" (1977, 15).

Agreement on any single equilibrium is problematic, because different equilibria imply different distributions of the net benefits of cooperation (Luce and Raiffa 1958, 121).[18] Although several game-theoretic solutions to this problem exist, no single solution currently commands

[16] Keohane's book, after all, is titled *AFTER Hegemony* (emphasis added) (1984).

[17] Lake advances an interesting explanation of this variation. He argues that whether an open system will be established varies as a function of its cost, that is, the price of its "infrastructure" and the magnitude of the side-payments necessary to persuade other states to adopt free trade (1988, 49–60).

[18] Snidal (1985b) does provide a good discussion of the distributional problems small groups encounter with respect to collective action generally.

general acceptance (Weingast and Marshall 1988, 170). Arguably more feasible solutions do exist.

As is true of firms attempting to cartelize, states can readily agree to maximize their joint profits or gains from trade if, one, the distribution of profits that results benefits all equally; or, two, side payments are possible. That collusion on the joint maximum will itself lead to an equal division of the gains from trade is unlikely. This will occur within an industrial cartel only in the highly improbable event that all firms are "absolutely" identical to each other (Friedman 1977, 28). In the context of international trade, it will occur only if reciprocal demand curves are identical in the negotiating countries—an equally improbable event.

The joint maximum theoretically retains its appeal if side payments are possible. Side payments redistribute the net benefits of cooperation among the relevant actors precisely in order to eliminate any inequities that arise as a result of their cooperation (Luce and Raiffa 1958, 180; see also Snidal 1985b, 605). Significant impediments to their use exist, however. The contracting parties must agree on a redistributive mechanism (Young 1975, 32n40); and, more importantly, recipients must accept the potential threat that inheres in their reliance on what is, in effect, the extension of subsidies to them from others. Oliver Williamson's assessment of the risks to subsidized firms applies as well to states:

> Firms which are authorized to expand relatively as a result of the agreement will be powerfully situated to demand a renegotiated settlement at a later date. Wary of such opportunism, firms for which retrenchment is indicated will decline from the outset to accept a full-blown profit-pooling arrangement. (1975, 224)

If neither natural nor induced symmetry of profit distribution renders the joint maximum a workable point of agreement, the "intrinsic magnetism of particular outcomes," as Thomas Schelling observes, may yet single out one member of the set of Pareto-improving equilibrium outcomes (cited in D. Baldwin 1987, 30). The "egalitarian nature" of the Swiss tariff-reduction proposal at the recently concluded Tokyo Round negotiations, for example, reportedly led to its general acceptance (Chan 1985, 463).

This example, however, perhaps illustrates more clearly the barriers to, than the possibilities of, the emergence of a unique "focal point" equilibrium. Behind agreement on equity as the standard for the Tokyo

Round formula stood the relatively equal power of the four principal parties to that negotiation, a long history of tariff cuts and a relatively low level of tariffs among them, and no discernible security ramifications to the accord.[19]

Absent any of these facilitating conditions, would-be international "k" groups may face insuperable obstacles to organization. The international context poses particularly difficult problems in this respect, as any distribution of the gains from trade can affect not only the economic but also the military balance of power among participating states. Thus, although the logic supporting the small-group criticism is unimpeachable, small groups in the international system confront some problems that do not plague hegemons.

Enforcement

Small-group proponents do attend closely to the problem of enforcement; they do not, however, resolve the problem. The discussion that follows focuses on the three hostages to good behavior in any single regime that are prominent in the small-group literature: Linkage to existing and, through reputations, to future regimes, and the breakdown of the regime in which the defection occurs (Keohane 1984, 100, 104–5).

The basis of the claim that linkage supplies an effective sanction is unclear. The small-group literature does not explain why exclusion from other existing regimes is a credible threat: It specifies neither the excludable goods they supply nor the cooperators' interests in punishing those who free ride on a *different* regime. As both theoretical and empirical analyses suggest, linkage may as easily torpedo as reinforce cooperation in any specific issue area. The interests of states in linking cooperation on one to cooperation on other issues can as easily diverge as converge.[20] Analytically, then, there is no reason to assume that linkage necessarily stabilizes cooperation.

Analogously, in order to attribute significant explanatory weight to reputation, small-group advocates must show, one, that extrapolations from past to future behavior are reliable because state interests do not

[19] That it was common knowledge the formula would not actually be applied uniformly across-the-board also helped. As Winham notes, "in the formula approach [to trade negotiations], nations tend to settle on as liberal a formula as possible, on the assumption that exceptions will be made for sensitive sectors when offers are actually tabled" (1986, 257).

[20] For discussion, see Oye (1979); Sebenius (1983); and Tollison and Willett (1979).

vary across time or situations; and, two, that informational asymmetries exist between the contracting parties.[21] Theoretical and empirical work on strategic deterrence, however, suggests that state interests and behavior do vary (Lebow 1985, 303–32). As a consequence, a state will not necessarily be able to rely upon the past to predict the behavior of another state in a different situation at a later time.

The regime context suggests that informational asymmetries will be rare. As Keohane (1984) has argued, regimes are created specifically to correct the "market-for-lemons" problem (i.e., situations in which informational asymmetries preclude the realization of gains from trade).[22] Because they supply information to states about the behavior of others, regimes do not provide opportunities for states to develop a reputation for honesty. As Robert H. Frank observes:

> if people act rationally, . . . we [cannot] discover that someone is honest by observing what he does in situations where the detection of cheating is not *unlikely*. . . . These are situations in which we frequently discover how a person has acted. For precisely this reason, however, it will not be rational to cheat in these cases. To observe that someone does not cheat would tell us only that he is prudent, not honest. . . . The kinds of actions that are likely to be observed are just not very good tests of whether a person is honest. (1988, 74–5, emphasis in original)

That states understand clearly the logic of Frank's argument is nicely illustrated by Lord Robert Salisbury's late-nineteenth-century comment about Prussian intentions: "That they should have been pacific when they were weak is not unnatural," he noted, "but if we wish to know the character of their disposition when left to itself, we must ask what they were when they were strong" (1870, 546).[23]

---

[21] It is this combination that motivates the role of reputations in such games as the chain-store paradox and formal analyses of cooperation in finite PDs. See Kreps and Wilson (1982); also Kreps et al. (1982).

[22] Moreover, any government known to put stock in past behavior invites others to cheat it. "The accumulation of a fund of goodwill of a buyer toward a seller that depends on past experience," as L. G. Telser observes, "stands as a ready temptation to the seller to cheat the buyers and convert their goodwill into ready cash." It is, Telser adds, "the prospect of the loss of future gain that deters and the existence of past goodwill that invites cheating." Therefore, he concludes, "rational behavior by the parties to an agreement requires that the probability of continuing their relation does not depend on their past experience with each other" (1980, 36).

[23] Lord Salisbury later became Britain's foreign minister and its prime minister. Between 1895 and 1900, he held both posts simultaneously.

In the abstract, at least, it may not matter much that these two hostages (linkage to existing regimes, and, via reputation, to future regimes) do not adequately secure cooperation. Sufficient power to deter free-riding inheres in the one mechanism to which the existing literature gives relatively short shrift: Each state's recognition that, "because regimes are difficult to construct, it may be rational to obey their rules if the alternative is their breakdown" (Keohane 1984, 100).[24] Endowed with additional structure, this recognition alone renders the cooperative a Nash or self-enforcing equilibrium.

If each state realizes that its attempt to free-ride will lead to the collapse of the regime, it has no incentive to defect, and the problem of enforcement does not arise. A critical omission in existing analyses, however, is how such a self-destruct mechanism might be built into a regime (Snidal 1985b, 610–11).

Clearly, a credible threat that the response to any attempt to free-ride will be the collapse of the entire regime creates just such a self-destruct mechanism. Existing work on tacit collusion among oligopolists relies on precisely this threat to stabilize cooperation. For example, all firms may agree to revert to the Cournot, or noncooperative, equilibrium for some period of time if *any* firm attempts to free-ride (Bendor and Mookherjee 1987; Yarbrough and Yarbrough 1986). The threat is credible because it is in every firm's interest to execute it, given that all others do so. By definition, if one firm believes that all other firms will, after any deviation, begin to produce their Cournot outputs, that firm cannot do better than do so itself (Friedman 1983, 131).[25] Thus, no firm has an interest in deviating from the collusive equilibrium: sanctions need never be implemented. This solution, then, is a self-enforcing agreement that can sustain cooperation without the need for recourse to linkage or to reputations.[26]

[24] Yarbrough and Yarbrough (1986, 7–22) discuss this solution briefly.

[25] The use of one such strategy to sustain cooperation in a PD game is discussed in more detail in Chapter Three. That discussion also makes clear that the threat of Cournot reversion is a subgame-perfect but is not a renegotiation-proof equilibrium strategy.

[26] Yarbrough and Yarbrough also suggest other mechanisms that can help secure free trade, for example, "a payment that changes hands contingent on compliance with the agreement." As they note, however, these mechanisms can require third-party adjudication because they create moral-hazard problems. A self-enforcing agreement "circumvents these problems and avoids a moral hazard by allowing the expected future benefits from continued compliance to serve as the bond. If a violation were falsely claimed, the agreement would end and the party falsely claiming grievance would lose" (1992, 79–80).

Application of this solution, of course, requires agreement among the contracting parties that a deviation has occurred, as well a consensus on the response to it. In the international system, however, not only the economic but also the political interests of states can influence judgments on these issues. Incentives to perceive and sanction a deviation can vary widely as the identity of the alleged deviant varies.

Free-riding, therefore, can occur. As Kindleberger observes, when "the police are politically opposed to a rule . . . or to its application in a given case," sanctioning becomes problematic. He adds that the history of the United Nations and the League of Nations before it demonstrates that attempts to protect the international collective good are highly vulnerable to the tendency of states to interpret any alleged threat to that good in highly self-interested ways.

Thus, a small group of states can encounter political problems in enforcing a cooperative equilibrium that do not confront hegemonic states.[27] In addition, as the next chapter suggests, groups vary with respect to their ability to resolve the enforcement problems that confront them. In particular, agreements among allies present fewer problems in this respect than do other interstate agreements: Incentives to deviate are weaker among allies; and, presumably, political conflicts of interest that can affect the sanctioning process are muted as well.

Conclusion

Although critics of hegemonic stability theory have not destroyed its analytic foundations, they have advanced the debate about it in unquestionably important ways. They have, for example, argued persuasively that a hegemonic preference for free trade cannot be assumed, that a more discriminating analysis is essential to establish the conditions under which a rational hegemon will, in its own interests, forgo an optimal tariff. In addition, they have forced a rigorous examination of the assumed public character of free trade. Moreover, they have successfully challenged the assumption that international public goods can be provided only by a single dominant state, and they have identified several of the system-level incentives and constraints that can influence the decisions of states about whether to open their borders

---

[27] Hegemonic enforcement can become problematic if its net costs become positive, however. For a detailed discussion, see Yarbrough and Yarbrough (1992).

to trade. They have made clear, for example, that the distribution of market power across states and the presence or absence of an effective deterrent to cheating play important roles.

Its critics have not, however, attacked the public-good variant of hegemonic stability theory at its point of maximum vulnerability. They have concentrated their fire on the trade preferences of a rational hegemon, the public-good attributes of free trade, and the ability of small groups to substitute for hegemons. They have not, however, targeted what is most problematic about the theory; it is markedly apolitical.

In one sense, hegemonic stability theory and the literature it inspired are about power. Indeed, the basic premise of the theory is that the distribution of power across states determines the probability that free trade will emerge in the world as a whole. And it is the particular constellation of power that hegemonic theory implicitly advocates that has drawn the fire of several of its most incisive critics.

In a more fundamental sense, this body of literature is genuinely apolitical. Although it assigns a central role to the distribution of power, it does so only in order to approximate the conditions conducive to the supply of public goods: A hegemonic state is the international analogue of a privileged group consisting of only one member. A small group of states is the international analogue of a "k" group. But the interest in power evident in debates about hegemonic stability theory is wholly derivative. Power matters only because some variants of its distribution are more conducive than others to the production of the public goods that must be supplied if free trade is to prevail.

The role hegemonic theory assigns to power, however, vitiates its essence—that is, the ability of one actor to influence the behavior of another. It is this aspect of the theory that reduces, if not eliminates, its intuitive appeal. Conversely, what enhances the appeal of explanations of the postwar economic order based on the Cold War is that they rely explicitly on the more conventional definition of power. In these explanations, the politics of trade most salient to the states engaged in it are the effects of trade on the balance of power among them.

This suggests that the relative dearth of free trade among nations over time may be a consequence of the play of great-power politics that an anarchic system induces. This, in turn, suggests that debates about hegemonic theory have neglected what may be the most durable barrier to free trade among the constituent great powers of any given international political system: that is, the primacy of concerns about security that characterize life in an anarchic world.

It is the failure of hegemonic stability theory to acknowledge and examine this barrier to trade that is its most profound flaw. Because of this and other flaws, hegemonic stability theory should be deposed from its position of prominence. Only a system-level theory that successfully redresses its most serious flaw can administer the coup de grâce.

In the next chapter, I begin to construct a Third-Image theory that takes explicitly into account the impact of the play of great-power politics on free trade.

Allies, Adversaries, and Free Trade

THIS CHAPTER CONTAINS the analytic core of the book. In it, I develop at length my argument about the impact of the anarchic structure of international politics on the exchange of goods and services among states. I cast my argument at the macroeconomic rather than microeconomic level. In other words, the argument advanced here is *not* about, for example, attempts to use economic statecraft to embargo exports of particular products or to inhibit the development of technologically advanced industries in other countries. It is instead an argument based on the effect of free trade on the real income and power potential of states.

I argue that strategic interaction among the great powers influences trade among them, because of the security externalities that trade produces. I consider these external effects explicitly. In order to do so, I construct and analyze a very simple game-theoretic model. The analysis makes clear that tariff games between allies differ systematically from those played between actual or potential adversaries.[1] These differences imply that free trade is more likely within than across political-military alliances. The analysis also suggests that alliances are more likely to evolve into free-trade coalitions if they are embedded in bipolar rather than multipolar systems.

The explanatory power of these hypotheses obviously depends directly on the incidence of alliances across nations and time. Less obviously, perhaps, it also depends on the attributes of the process of alliance-formation. In my analysis, I assume that rational-choice theory can explain intra-alliance trade patterns. This assumption makes sense only if closely related decisions—that is, decisions about alliance entry—can also be understood as the outcome of a rational-choice process.

As a result, in the first section of this chapter, I examine the extent

[1] Tariffs are used here as a substitute for all forms of government intervention in trade. Because of constraints imposed by GATT, intervention now usually takes the form of nontariff barriers to trade (NTBs). As long as the home country captures the scarcity rents that accrue from trade barriers, the form in which intervention occurs does not affect the argument presented here.

to which the anarchic structure of the international system induces rational states to ally with each other. Then I develop in detail my argument about the impact of great-power politics on inter-state trade.

A RATIONAL-CHOICE THEORY OF ALLIANCE FORMATION

I define an alliance in conventional terms, that is, as "a formal agreement between two or more nations to collaborate on national security issues" (Holsti, Hopmann, and Sullivan 1973, 4).[2] At least three different types of alliances exist: (1) a defense pact, which commits its signatories "to intervene militarily on behalf of one another"; (2) a neutrality or nonaggression pact, which obligates the parties to it to remain neutral in the event of war; and (3) an entente, which mandates consultation and/or cooperation if a war occurs (Small and Singer 1969).

The frequency with which great-power alliances have formed over time and across nations suggests that there is nothing puzzling about these alliances. They seem to be an inevitable concomitant of life in an anarchic world. Absent any supranational authority, states exist in a self-help system. In such a system, unless a state can ensure its security unilaterally, it will ally with others in order to do so. The net effect is to maintain the balance of power in the international system as a whole. It is this logic that led Hans J. Morgenthau, for example, to assert that the "most important manifestation of the balance of power" inheres "in the relations between one nation or alliance of nations and another alliance" ([1948] 1973, 181).

Recent literature tends to refine, rather than challenge, the claim about the relationship between system structure and alliance-formation that Morgenthau and others advanced long ago. Stephen M. Walt, for example, argues that it is the balance of threat rather than the balance of power that motivates states to ally with each other (1987).[3] Walt (1987, 1989); Thomas J. Christensen and Jack Snyder (1990); and Conybeare

[2] Bruce Russett defines an alliance in very similar terms: that is, as "*a formal agreement among a limited number of countries concerning the conditions under which they will or will not employ military force*") (1971, 262–63, emphasis in original). Glenn Snyder does so as well. Alliances, he observes, "are formal associations of states for the use (or nonuse) of military force, intended for either the security or the aggrandizement of their members, against specific other nations" (1990, 104). Walt, however, contends that alliances can also be based on tacit rather than on explicit agreements (1987, 12).

[3] For incisive critiques of Walt's argument, see Keohane (1988) and G. Snyder (1991).

(1992), among others, have examined the pre- and post-entry strategy sets available to states, while James D. Morrow (1991) has examined the objectives of alliance entry.[4] Although each of these studies is important in its own right, none of them supplants the claim that alliances are a consequence of a balance-of-power world.

The same statement can be made about attempts to analyze alliance-formation more rigorously than was typical of early literature in the field (e.g., Liska 1962; Holsti, Hopman, and Sullivan 1973). Glenn Snyder, for example, models the process as a PD game.[5] He argues that PD-preference orderings characterize states confronting decisions about whether to seek allies, because "(1) some states may not be satisfied with only moderate security, and they can increase it substantially by allying if others abstain [i.e., $T > R$]; [and] (2) some states, fearing that others will not abstain, will ally in order to avoid isolation or to preclude the partner from allying against them [i.e., $P > S$]" (1984, 462).

Because alliance entry is a dominant strategy, Snyder continues, alliances inevitably populate international systems. This outcome is collectively suboptimal, however; "if all states are about equally strong and are interested only in security, all are fairly well off if all abstain, since each has moderate security against individual others," while alliances "involve various costs, such as reduced freedom of action, commitments to defend the interests of others, and so forth" (Snyder 1984, 462).

Thus, although Snyder formalizes conventional arguments about alliance formation, he does not challenge their underlying logic. As is true of other recent contributors to the literature on alliances, he tends to accept the long-standing argument that alliances are the product of anarchic systems and of concerns about the balance of power that such systems induce.

The process of alliance-formation, however, *is* intrinsically problem-

---

[4] A variety of candidate strategies exist. Walt, for example, argues that states seeking allies can either balance or bandwagon; that is, they can choose to ally with or against the threatening state (1987; 1989). Conybeare argues that one determinant of pre-alliance entry strategies is an attempt to maximize a "combination of risk and return" (1992). The relevant strategy set available to states that have already entered into an alliance, suggest Christensen and Snyder, includes "chain-ganging" and "buck-passing" (that is, offering an ally an irrevocable rather than an easily reversible commitment) (1990).

[5] Niou, Ordeshook, and Rose (1989) formalize the process of alliance-formation, but they rely on cooperative game theory to do so. As a result, as G. Snyder argues, the empirical relevance of their argument is limited (1991, 132).

atic. Indeed, within the context of balance-of-power theory, alliance-formation is paradoxical. Balance-of-power theory implies, as Arthur A. Stein observes, that states concerned with their own survival will

> act in concert to prevent the emergence of a power that threatens them. This coincidence of interests forms the basis for alliances, which in turn undergird a balance of power. Hence these alliances hardly seem necessary. If, on the other hand, alliances entail commitments that states have no interest in fulfilling, then nations will not keep to their terms, and the accords will have no consequences. Alliances, then, must be either unnecessary or inherently unbelievable bluffs.[6] (1990, 153)

The logic of Stein's argument is compelling. Two interests presumably motivate a state to enter into an alliance.[7] One interest is to increase a state's ability to deter war.[8] Another is to enhance its ability to prevail if a war occurs. If alliance commitments are problematic, however, alliances will neither enhance deterrence nor increase the probability of prevailing in the event of war.

Alliance commitments are almost always problematic. It is very difficult for any state to credibly commit to enter a future war in which its ally is a belligerent. Indeed, if only an imperfect congruence of interests between allies exists, the temptation to renege in the event of war may prove irresistible.[9] If such postcontractual opportunism is plausible and its existence is common knowledge, alliances will not

[6] Stein is not the first or only scholar to have made this point. Morgenthau, for example, noted that when the interests of states are such that they "obviously call for concerted policies and actions . . . [then] an explicit formulation of these interests, policies, and actions in the form of a treaty of alliance appears to be redundant" (1948 [1973], 182). For another example, see Morrow (1991, 906).

[7] Paul Schroeder (1976) has argued that states also enter alliances in order to control the behavior of their allies. This interest is not distinct from those discussed in the text, however; presumably the ultimate objective of such control is to win or deter a war.

[8] As Lalman and Newman have pointed out, however, an alliance can also have an unintended, opposite effect. Because a state's entry into an alliance reveals "which nations are friendly enough for alliance partners, a nation also reveals which nations are not as close. This new information may prove risky to a nation's efforts to deter threats" (1991, 242).

[9] This is precisely the problem that plagued NATO during the Cold War. Despite the declared commitment of the United States to its European allies, it was clear to them that their interests and those of the United States did not coincide completely. For example, that the United States would elect to risk nuclear war with the U.S.S.R. in the event of a Soviet attack on Western Europe always seemed less than certain to the European allies of the United States.

have significant effects either on deterrence or on the probability of victory.[10] Under these circumstances, no state will have a strong incentive to ally with any other.

That alliances are neither uncommon nor omnipresent in the real world suggests, however, that they are neither inevitable *nor* worthless by-products of anarchic international systems. Even if the assumption that the alliance entry game is a PD is maintained, Glenn Snyder's conclusion does not necessarily follow. There is nothing inevitable about the outcome of an infinitely repeated PD game or of a finite game in which incomplete information exists. Under either condition, strategic interaction between or among states engaged in such a game *can* produce an alliance-free international system.[11]

If the assumption about PD preferences is not maintained, it is much more difficult to sustain the claim that alliance-formation is inevitable. State preferences with respect to alliances, for example, might conform to those that define the game of Harmony. As figure 3.1 makes clear, alliance abstention (cooperation) is a dominant strategy in this game. Each state is better off if it does *not* ally, whether or not another state chooses to do so.

There are several situations that might induce this preference ranking. Among them is one in which all great powers are satisfied with the international status quo and their preferences are common knowledge. The Concert of Europe seems to be an example, even if relatively brief, of such a situation.[12] As suggested by recent developments within the former Soviet Union and between it and the United States, a dominant

[10] The empirical evidence is mixed about the extent to which states honor their commitments to their allies in the event of war. Siverson and King argue, for example, that although "many alliance partners joined in war participation (67 or 23.1 percent) [between 1815 and 1965], many more (223 or 76.9 percent) did not" (1980, 2). Bruce Bueno de Mesquita, however, argues that, of nations which were attacked, "76 percent of the allied nations received fighting support from *some* of their allies, while only 17 percent of the nonallied states found anyone fighting alongside them" (1981, 113, emphasis added).

Note that Bueno de Mesquita's calculation addresses only the issue of whether a belligerent received support from *some* of its allies. It does not address what seems to be the more relevant question; that is, the percentage of a belligerent's allies that honored their commitment to enter the relevant war.

[11] It is important to note that iteration does not ensure that the Pareto-superior equilibrium outcome will emerge. The only equilibrium outcome of the stage game (that is, PP) is also an equilibrium outcome of the repeated game. The effect of iteration on PD games is explained in more detail later in this chapter.

[12] For an incisive analysis of the operation of the Concert, see Jervis (1985).

Column

Cooperate   Defect

	Cooperate	Defect
Cooperate	4,4	2,3
Defect	3,2	1,1

Row

FIGURE 3.1. Harmony

strategy equilibrium of alliance abstention might also emerge as a consequence of the disintegration of one or more great powers.[13]

Thus, the argument of G. Snyder and others that alliance-formation is inevitable is not persuasive. Neither is the argument that, because alliances are necessarily "cheap talk," alliance entry is irrational. If, for example, information is incomplete, and if costly signaling accompanies alliance formation, alliances may not be inherently incredible bluffs.[14] Stein himself is sensitive to this possibility. Even if alliances do not actually influence the behavior of the allied states, he observes, they "may still fulfill a useful role as devices to signal to third parties intentions about contingent future behavior that might otherwise not be presumptive" (1990, 153n7).

Reputational effects, for example, can induce a state to enter a war in which its ally is a belligerent even if that state expects to incur short-run costs in doing so *and* the outcome of the war will not directly affect its interests. Although a state might be better off in the short run if it reneges on its commitment to its ally, it may be better off in the long run if it does not. If it reneges, a state may acquire a reputation as an unreliable ally.[15] Thus, the long-run reputational costs which a state

[13] States can also abjure alliances if their preferences conform to those that define an Assurance Game; that is, $R > T > P > S$.

[14] "To reveal private information where there are incentives to misrepresent it," as James Fearon observes, "signals must be costly in a quite specific way. For example, in crisis bargaining an action that is equally costly to take whether the state has high or low resolve should not lead a rational adversary to change its prior belief about the state's true willingness to use force." Rather, he adds, "only actions that are potentially *more* costly for 'low resolve' than for 'high resolve' states will convey willingness to use force on the particular issues in dispute" (1992, 38; emphasis in original).

[15] In a footnote, Stein does refer to the possibility that a state might honor its commitment to an ally if it is concerned about its reputation (1990, 164n44). Conybeare also

incurs if it reneges may exceed those of entering the war. Treaties, as Charles Lipson observes, put "reputation at stake." As a result, he notes, they "add to the costs of breaking agreements, or rather, they do so if a signatory values reputation" (1991, 533).

The existence of incomplete information about either state types or interests, however, is not necessary to explain alliance formation in a balance-of-power world. Rational states may ally with each other even if their interests are wholly congruent *and* this congruence is common knowledge. They might do so, for example, if the formation of an alliance facilitates either the exploitation of economies of scale with respect to defense and deterrence or the ex ante coordination of strategies that is essential to maximize the probability of victory in the event of war.[16]

The North Atlantic Treaty Organization seems to be an example of such a case. NATO has enabled its members to exploit the scale economies that inhere in nuclear weapons, as well as coordinate their wartime strategies ex ante.[17] A less obvious example is the Anglo-French Entente. The pre–World War I accord between Britain and France allowed its members to coordinate their forces ex ante insofar as the accord entailed an implicit division of labor with respect to naval power in the event of war with Germany.

The formation of alliances is, in short, more problematic than much of the international relations literature suggests. Decisions to ally are not inevitable, even if state preferences conform to those that characterize a PD game. Nor are alliances necessarily a credible deterrent to war. Nonetheless, a rational state may adopt a strategy of alliance entry for any of several reasons: to allow it to signal its interests to other states in situations of incomplete information; to exploit economies of scale with respect to deterrence and/or defense; or to effect the ex ante coordination of forces that might influence the outcome of any war that does occur.[18]

---

notes that unreliable allies "would suffer reputational and possibly other sanctions, leaving them dangerously isolated" (1992, 65n8).

[16] The presence or absence of potential welfare gains from explicit coordination may answer one question Keohane raises in his review of Walt's book: "Under what conditions do alliances become formalized?" (1988, 175).

[17] This is obviously not meant to imply that the members of NATO have identical stakes in all situations, nor that economies of scale exist or have been exploited with respect to all the military forces of NATO's members.

[18] Altfeld (1984) argues for and provides an empirical test of the hypothesis that ra-

Decisions to ally, therefore, *can* be understood as the product of strategic interaction among rational states. This suggests that it makes sense to assess the impact of alliances on trade within the context of an analytic framework based on the same assumption: that is, that states act rationally. The next section of this chapter focuses explicitly on the question of the conditions under which rational states will trade more freely within than across alliances.

POWER, TRADE, AND TARIFFS

The play of great-power politics affects the incentives of states to trade freely with each other because of the security externalities associated with trade. These external effects arise because the source of gains from trade is the increased efficiency with which domestic resources can be employed. The resulting increase in real income frees economic resources for military uses. Thus, trade increases the potential military power of any country that engages in it (D. Baldwin 1985, 216; Hirschman [1945] 1980, 14; McKeown 1982; Root 1984, 75; Srinivasan 1987, 352).

The anarchic structure of the international system implies, in turn, that a state cannot be indifferent to the potential power of either its allies or its adversaries. Inherent in the structure of the international system is the ability of any state to use or threaten to use military force to achieve its goals. Whether any state will do so depends in part on its power. The latter depends in part on its real income. As a result, any increase in the real income of its adversaries decreases the security of a state. Conversely, increases in the income of its allies increase its own security.[19]

Thus, the real income gains that motivate free trade are the source of the externalities that can either impede or facilitate it: Trade with

---

tional states will join alliances if, for example, the opportunity costs of doing so are lower than are those involved in a unilateral increase in military spending. Morrow (1991) argues and finds empirical support for the proposition that states trade off security gains against autonomy losses when they ally.

[19] As Srinivasan points out, whether a state will actually use its gains from trade to increase its defense budget depends on its social-welfare function (1987, 356–57). This does not affect the analysis here because, if conditions change, increased GNP will allow a state to increase its military power more easily than it would otherwise have been able to do.

an adversary produces a security diseconomy; trade with an ally produces a positive externality. In either case, trade creates a divergence between private and social costs: The costs of trade to the nation differ from those that accrue to the individuals involved.[20] This implies that government intervention in trade can increase the welfare of the nation as a whole.

Government Intervention in Trade: "Acupuncture with a Fork?"

The argument I advance here joins a relatively large set of arguments for government intervention in trade that are based on national security. This argument is *not,* however, vulnerable to the logical flaw that afflicts many members of this set. In most cases, careful analysis leads ineluctably to the conclusion that intervention in trade is only rarely, if ever, the optimal response to situations in which trade adversely affects national security.

The situations can be diverse. For example, they can involve the impact of free trade on the industrial structure of a nation, on the composition of its labor force, or on its pattern of consumption. The diversity of situations does not change the well-established conclusion that intervention in trade imposes higher costs on national welfare than do other policy alternatives.

The logic of the argument that leads to this conclusion is straightforward. Suppose, for example, that open international markets result in a pattern of domestic production that is inimical to national defense. More specifically, suppose that free trade leads to a socially suboptimal level of production in certain industries. A market failure results: Private and social costs of production diverge. As a consequence, government intervention can correct this distortion and thereby increase national welfare.

Intervention in trade, however, is not the most efficient response to a market failure of this kind. A tariff can raise output in the affected industries to the socially optimal level. Because it does so by increasing domestic prices, the tariff simultaneously distorts consumption. A production subsidy is a more efficient response. It raises output to the optimal level without influencing prices. An analogous argument would apply if, for example, consumption were either above or below the socially optimal level. A consumption tax or subsidy would correct the

[20] See Chapter One, note 9, for an explanation of why externalities create a divergence between private and social returns.

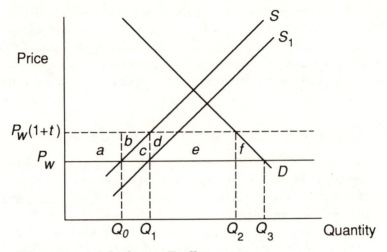

FIGURE 3.2.   A Subsidy vs. a Tariff
Source: Deardorff and Stern 1987, 35.

market failure without the adverse effect on production that would result from a tariff.

Figure 3.2 illustrates this argument. The figure depicts the domestic
market for a good that can also be imported at the world price, P_w. Free
trade, however, leads to a socially suboptimal level of domestic output,
Q_0, in a particular industry. S represents the private marginal cost, and
S_1 the social marginal cost of producing the good. The social benefit
that would accrue from an increase in output is measured by the area
between the two curves. In addition to its usual effects, therefore, a
tariff that increases domestic output from Q_0 to Q_1 also generates social
benefits equal to the area of $b + c$. If b is greater than f, a tariff increases
welfare.

A production subsidy, however, achieves the same result at less cost.
The subsidy costs the government $a + b + c$. Part of this subsidy, $a +
b$, is a transfer to producers; but part of it is a social gain, $b + c$. The
net gain, therefore, is equal to b. Because $b > b - f$, a production subsidy
is welfare-superior to a tariff. The general principle, as Alan V. Deardorff and Robert M. Stern observe,

> is that trade intervention, by introducing two distortions rather than one,
> may succeed in solving one problem but only at the same time that it
> causes another. Trade policy is like doing acupuncture with a fork: no

matter how carefully you insert one prong, the other is likely to do damage. (1987, 39)

Thus, in most cases in which free trade adversely affects national security, the first-best policy is not trade intervention but a policy that deals with the divergence directly (Corden 1986, 86)—production subsidies if domestic production is judged inadequate, consumption taxes or subsidies if consumption is above or below socially optimal levels, wage subsidies if market forces lead to socially suboptimal levels of employment for workers who possess skills perceived as essential for national security.

A first-best case for tariffs as a response to market failure remains, however, where the distortion originates in trade itself. An embargo is perhaps the most obvious case. If the probability of a trade embargo is an increasing function of the volume of imports *and* this relationship is not recognized by private traders, a trade distortion exists: The social cost of imports is higher than is their private cost. In this situation, the optimal policy choice can be a tariff (Bhagwati and Srinivasan, 1976).[21]

Even a credible embargo threat requires government intervention if and only if private markets do not anticipate and respond to the threat. However, strong incentives to anticipate an embargo and to react appropriately confront individual traders in the market concerned. They can, for example, use "furnaces that can switch from oil to gas or viceversa, cultivate a more diverse clientele for exports, maintain other sources of supply (including stockpiles), and so forth" (Dixit 1987, 267). As a consequence, even a credible embargo threat does not always create a role for preemptive action by the government.[22]

In sum, it seems difficult to defend successfully any claim that intervention in trade is the first-best response to situations in which free trade adversely affects national security. Whether the market failure involves an inadequate level of domestic production, insufficient or excessive domestic consumption, or an inadequate supply of workers with particular skills, avoiding "acupuncture with a fork" implies correcting the distortion at the source rather than intervening in trade. With the possible exception of an embargo that does not prompt action

[21] For a dissenting view about the relationship between import volume and the probability of an embargo, see Helpman (1987, 372).

[22] When it does, in addition, several policy alternatives exist that are less costly than import restrictions (for example, supplying information to private traders about prospective embargoes, accumulating stockpiles, imposing consumption taxes, and providing production subsidies) (Dixit 1987, 265).

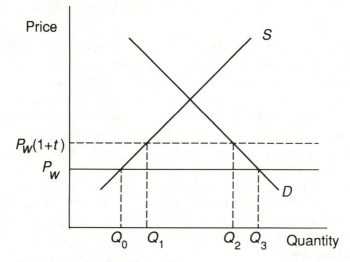

FIGURE 3.3. Trade with an Adversary

by private markets, trade intervention can be justified only as a second-best response.

This conclusion does *not* apply to the argument of this book, that trade between adversaries creates security diseconomies. In this case, the market failure does not originate in a domestic distortion; it originates in trade itself. In addition, unlike an embargo, this situation does not create strong incentives for private markets to respond appropriately. An individual trader will have an incentive to take these social costs into account only in the unlikely event that his trade is very large relative to the nation's as a whole. As a consequence, only government intervention can correct the divergence between private and social costs that arises as a consequence of the security externalities associated with trade. Moreover, because the marginal divergence arises as a direct consequence of trade, intervention in trade is a first-best policy. Figure 3.3 illustrates this situation.

The figure shows the domestic market for a good that can also be imported at its world price, P_w, which is the private marginal cost of imports. In the absence of government intervention, domestic output is Q_0; domestic demand is Q_3; and the amount imported is the difference between them $(Q_3 - Q_0)$. Because of the external diseconomy that trade with actual or potential adversaries generates, the marginal social cost of imports is higher, shown as $P_w(1 + t)$. This market failure can be eliminated by a tariff, t, which increases domestic prices to P_w (1 + t); raises domestic output to Q_1, lowers domestic demand to Q_2, and reduces imports to $Q_2 - Q_1$. In this case, "acupuncture with a fork" *is* the treatment of choice. Restricting trade both by raising the price of imports and by expanding domestic production is optimal.

Optimal Tariff Games

Successful intervention in trade, to correct the security externalities associated with it, depends on the ability of a country to affect the real income of the state which is its target. Although any tariff will distort resource allocation in the target country and therefore decrease its real income, it will do so without imposing net costs on the home country only if the latter can affect its terms of trade (i.e., the relative price of its exports on world markets).

One of the principal lessons of standard trade theory is that the ability of a state to influence its terms of trade depends on its size in global markets. Standard theory also makes clear, it should be noted, that the relevant size is not that "of the country as a whole but rather its share of world trade in markets in which it exports and imports" (Deardorff and Stern 1987, 37). If a country is large enough to exercise market power, then, it can use a tariff to increase its own real income at its adversary's expense.[23] In doing so, it will narrow the gap between the private and social costs of trade. Thus, a tariff can be welfare-superior to a policy of free trade for a state in an anarchic international political system.

Under the assumptions of standard international trade theory, an optimal tariff is the *only* alternative available to a country that seeks to reduce the income of its trading partner without incurring a net reduction in its own.[24] However, strategic trade theory, developed recently, suggests that other instruments of trade policy can achieve the same end.[25] It does so because, unlike its predecessor, strategic trade theory does not assume that perfect competition prevails in all markets.

[23] In order to do so without imposing costs on its allies, a country must be able to use discriminatory trade policies. This is not easy to accomplish. For detailed analyses, see Willett and Jalalighajar (1983–84); Bayard, Pelzman, and Lopez (1983); and Kaempfer and Lowenberg (1992).

[24] For a complete explanation of the assumptions that standard trade theory relies upon, see Yarbrough and Yarbrough (1991, 280–81).

[25] The seminal article in this area is Brander and Spencer (1984).

Instead, strategic trade theory assumes that some industries are more valuable than are others to the nation as a whole. If such industries exist, government intervention in trade can increase national welfare. As in the case of standard trade theory, such intervention will decrease the real income of the target country.

The logic of strategic trade theory is straightforward. The basic assumption is that some industries generate excess profits or rents—that is, "a receipt in excess of the opportunity cost of a resource" (Ekelund and Tollison 1981, 18).[26] A nation can therefore increase its real income to the extent that it can capture a larger share of these profits. Under carefully specified conditions, government intervention in the form of an export subsidy will enable it to do so.[27] The subsidy allows the home industry to credibly commit to producing a larger output than it would otherwise, thereby forcing its foreign rival to contract its output.[28] Because the increase in home industry profits that results exceeds the amount of the subsidy, national welfare rises.[29]

Government intervention in trade can also be welfare-enhancing in the case of industries that generate externalities.[30] When an industry

[26] These returns "can be thought of as scarcity values of the restricted positions or slots in the industry. . . . [Thus,] economists call them monopoly rents" (Dixit 1986, 290).

[27] For example, although the existence of excess profits is a prerequisite for a welfare-enhancing export subsidy, it is difficult to establish whether industries are actually generating rents. Concentration among firms in an industry is not sufficient by itself to imply that excess profits exist, because competition may be fierce even if the number of firms is small (Dixit 1986, 292). In addition, supranormal profits at the end stage of competition may follow subnormal profits at the initial period, thus making average returns normal (Dixit, cited in Richardson 1987, 287).

Moreover, the existence of excess profits is necessary but not sufficient to ensure that an export subsidy will increase national welfare. Among other necessary conditions are: (1) the industry itself cannot capture these profits (Dixit 1986, 294); (2) the competition between the targeted industry and its rival is Cournot rather than Bertrand (that is, the strategic variable is output rather than price); and (3) the number of domestic firms in the relevant industry is small. If price competition exists or the number of domestic firms is large, an export subsidy will decrease rather than increase national welfare: An export tax is indicated instead (Eaton and Grossman 1983).

[28] More precisely, the subsidy empowers the home industry to act as a Stackelberg leader. As such, the home industry can determine where on its reaction curve its rival will operate.

[29] The impact on consumer surplus is not at issue here. The Brander–Spencer model assumes that industry output is not consumed at home. As a result, the effect on consumer surplus does not enter the welfare calculations of the subsidizing country.

[30] Again, intervention on the basis of externalities will enhance welfare only if certain conditions are met. For example, externalities must be country-specific. Externalities,

generates positive externalities, its output is socially suboptimal. Although its operation does not necessarily produce supranormal profits in the form of direct returns to factors employed in the industry, "capital and labor in the sector . . . will yield high returns to society because in addition to their own earnings they provide benefits to capital and labor employed elsewhere" (Krugman 1986, 13). One source of externalities, for example, inheres in the incomplete appropriability of new knowledge: Frequently, it is difficult to prevent others from benefiting from the creation of knowledge; as a result, private markets tend to underinvest in it.

For several reasons, I base the analysis in this book upon standard, rather than strategic, trade theory. First, it is standard trade theory that underlies much of the analytic literature in the subfield of international political economy. Second, strategic trade theory was not developed until after 1980, although it is, of course, conceivable that policymakers had an intuitive appreciation of strategic trade theory that preceded its formalization. Third, the advent of strategic trade theory does not affect the logic of the argument I advance here. Its only effect is to expand the range of policy instruments to which it can be applied. For these reasons and in order to simplify the presentation, I base the following analysis on standard trade theory.

Thus, I argue that countries can use their ability to affect their terms of trade to correct the market failure produced by trade in an anarchic system. This is, of course, a variant of the traditional optimal tariff argument.[31] As such, it might elicit the same skepticism that greets this and other suggestions about using trade policy as a rent-seeking instrument.[32] In addition, the fatal weakness of the conventional optimal

---

however, often cross borders (for example, via the diffusion of knowledge or trade in intermediate goods) (Krugman 1987, 231). Indeed, if an externality is international, optimal policy is to free-ride on the subsidies of *other* nations (Dixit 1987, 266).

In addition, external economies are unpriced. As a result, Krugman contends that governments can identify industries that are potential targets of welfare-increasing intervention only by combining "detailed knowledge of the industry with a heavy reliance on guesswork" (1986, 17). Others are somewhat more sanguine. Richardson argues that "indicators" of the value of externalities can be observed, such as "the renewal patterns of license fees for patents, the different valuations of a firm by the stock market and its takeover suitor, and the subtly conditioned covariation in productivity growth across different economic activities" (1990, 119).

[31] Chapter Two provides a more detailed explanation of the optimal tariff argument.

[32] See, for example, Deardorff and Stern (1987, 34).

tariff argument seems to afflict the argument presented here. If retaliation ensues, both states will be worse off: the volume of trade will decrease, but the terms of trade will not change.[33] The optimal tariff game, in short, is a PD game.

The novelty of the argument in this book inheres in its conclusions about the PD games that result when states simultaneously attempt to exert power over their terms of trade. The discussion that follows demonstrates that tariff games between allies differ systematically from those that actual or potential adversaries play. It also suggests that the probability that alliances will evolve into free-trade coalitions varies across international systems.

THE STANDARD OPTIMAL TARIFF GAME

The payoff matrix of the standard optimal tariff game is shown in figure 3.4. In this variant of the PD game, T represents the payoff that accrues to a state that unilaterally deploys an optimal tariff. R is the payoff to each state if both trade freely with each other. P is the return that accrues if both use optimal tariffs. And S is the payoff to unilateral free trade.

In any finitely repeated game, defection is a dominant strategy. As a result, the inevitable outcome of any such game is bilateral tariffs.[34] In contrast, in a game in which states assume at every period that there is some positive probability that the game will continue, a variety of Pareto-improving outcomes, including that of free trade, can be realized.[35]

This can occur, for example, if both states adopt a "grim" strategy: that is, begin with free trade (i.e., cooperation). Then, trade freely in the succeeding period if the other cooperated in the previous period; otherwise, deploy an optimal tariff (i.e., defect).[36] This strategy will sus-

---

[33] This assumes that states possess identical degrees of market power. If they do not, it is possible for one state to be better off even after the cycle has been completed than if it had pursued free trade. See Johnson (1953–54, 142–53).

[34] As noted above, if incomplete information of a specific kind exists in a finite PD game, it is possible for mutual cooperation to emerge on at least some plays of the game. See Kreps et al. (1982).

[35] As the folk theorem states, if the horizon is infinite and the actors are very patient, *any* individually rational outcome can be sustained (Fudenberg and Maskin 1986).

[36] In a context in which deviations are perfectly observable, maximal punishment makes sense, because it never occurs on the equilibrium path. It is, therefore, costless (Tirole 1988, 252). Moreover, unlike Tit for Tat (Axelrod 1984), a grim strategy is

Column

	Cooperate	Defect

		Cooperate	R,R	S,T
Row				
	Defect	T,S	P,P

FIGURE 3.4. The Standard Optimal Tariff Game
Note: $T > R > P > S$; $R \geqslant (T + S)/2$

tain cooperation in a PD game if the discounted sum of cooperative payoffs, $R/(1 - \delta)$, is greater than is the sum of the one-shot gain from defection, T, and the discounted sum of punishment payoffs, $\delta P/(1 - \delta)$.[37] Thus, cooperation can be sustained by a grim strategy if:

$$\frac{R}{(1 - \delta)} \geqslant T + \frac{\delta P}{(1 - \delta)}$$

or

$$\delta \geqslant \frac{(T - R)}{(T - P)} \tag{3.1}$$

If this incentive-compatibility constraint is satisfied, a grim strategy will enable free trade to emerge as the outcome of an infinite-horizon optimal tariff game. The success of the General Agreement on Tariffs and Trade suggests that this is possible not only in the abstract but also

---

subgame-perfect; that is, it is rational for the players to follow the specified strategies if any defection occurs (Rasmusen 1989, 91).

It is not renegotiation-proof, however. That is, if one player defects and the players have the opportunity to renegotiate, they will abandon the punishment strategy in favor of one that confers higher payoffs. A Pareto-perfect or weakly renegotiation-proof strategy is a "penance" strategy: Begin with cooperation; if a deviation occurs, the deviator cooperates and the other player defects; the players then revert to cooperation (Fudenberg and Tirole 1991, 179–82). I use a grim strategy here for two reasons: (1) it is more accessible and, more importantly; (2) the results of the analysis do not change if a penance strategy is used.

[37] The discount factor, δ, reflects both the rate of time preference, ρ, and the probability that the game will end, θ. The discount factor is $(1 - \theta)/(1 + \rho)$ (Rasmusen 1989, 90).

State j

	Cooperate	Defect
Cooperate	$R_i \text{-} w_{ij} R_j, R_j \text{-} w_{ji} R_i$	$S_i \text{-} w_{ij} T_j, T_j \text{-} w_{ji} S_i$
Defect	$T_i \text{-} w_{ij} S_j, S_j \text{-} w_{ji} T_i$	$P_i \text{-} w_{ij} P_j, P_j \text{-} w_{ji} P_i$

State i (Cooperate / Defect rows)

FIGURE 3.5. The Prisoners' Dilemma: Adversaries
   Note: This payoff matrix omits second-order effects.

in the real world. Established in 1947, the GATT was created to (and did) enable states to avoid a replay of the tariff game that stymied trade among them in the interwar period.[38]

TARIFF GAMES BETWEEN ADVERSARIES

The payoff matrix of the standard optimal tariff game assumes that private and social returns to interstate trade do not differ. Life in an anarchic international system, however, effectively alters the payoffs of the standard game. Because interstate trade in such a system produces externalities, this trade creates a divergence between private and social returns that any utility-maximizing state will take into account when it calculates its payoffs from trade.

Thus, the payoffs a state assigns to the outcomes of any given trade game differ from those of the standard optimal tariff matrix. In the case of trade with an adversary, a state incurs a marginal social cost that the standard matrix does not reflect. This transforms the standard matrix as shown in figure 3.5. In each cell, the marginal social cost that a state, i, incurs is represented as a fraction, w_{ij}, of the payoff that accrues to its adversary, j.[39] Thus, $w_{ij}R_j$, for example, is the marginal social cost or security diseconomy that accrues to state i when it trades freely with state j.

[38] Even though much progress has been made, completely free trade remains elusive. Nonetheless, GATT has clearly facilitated the process of lowering trade barriers among its member countries. Yarbrough and Yarbrough argue that it is neither grim nor any other self-enforcing strategies but third party (U.S.) enforcement that has deterred states from defecting from GATT agreements (1992, 42).

[39] Here, w is assumed to be a constant in order to simplify the presentation. The effect of allowing w to vary across trading partners is discussed in Chapter Six.

This cost is represented as an increasing function of the adversary's gains from trade. The representation is based in part on what Robert Powell has described as a "very simple, highly stylized assumption about the nature of warfare." That is, the "stronger a state is economically, the more likely it is to prevail in war" (1991, 1,312). Although it is not conclusive, of course, the experience of both twentieth-century world wars suggests that this assumption does not depend on abstract reasoning alone. In each case, the aggregate economic output of the belligerent states was a powerful determinant of the outcome of the war (Kennedy 1985).

The functional dependence of social on private returns from trade also has a microeconomic, or sector-specific, component. The increase in domestic resource efficiency that results from trade frees economic resources for military uses. Whether resource diversion to the military will actually occur depends upon the income elasticity of demand for military spending. If military goods are "normal" goods, the income elasticity of demand for them will be positive. Whether or not they are normal goods obviously depends on state preferences. If, for example, a state engaged in an arms race has preferences that conform to a Deadlock game, it is very probable that its arms will increase as its income does. PD preferences make this less likely but by no means impossible.[40] Historically, however, income and military spending have been directly related.[41]

I assume, then, that the marginal social cost that state i incurs when it trades with its adversary, j, is directly related to the gains from trade of the latter. Although it is not strictly necessary to the analysis, I also assume that w_{ij} is less than 1; that is, I assume that the marginal social cost associated with trade is only a fraction of the gains from trade that accrue to the adversarial state.[42] I do so because military portfolios reflect the diversified interests of great powers. Typically, any great power has a range of security interests, only some of which affect the interests of another great power. Its portfolio of military weapons will reflect

[40] For an incisive, extended discussion of this issue, see Downs and Rocke (1990, 68–79).

[41] Klaus Knorr has observed that "absolute amounts of military spending are, on the whole, closely correlated with GNP" (1977, 184).

[42] The effect of allowing w to equal 1 would be to eliminate trade between adversaries, because the resulting game would no longer be a PD. Thus, the logic of the argument would not be affected, but the findings would change. See note 44 below.

49

these interests. Because military resources are not completely fungible, not all additions to the military power of an adversary will disadvantage its trading partner. Thus, even if an adversary did divert all of its gains from trade to the military sector, its action would not necessarily inflict a social cost on its trading partner equal to the incremental addition to its military power.

For example, many resources that the United States deployed to prosecute the Vietnam War would not have been useful in either a conventional or a nuclear war with the Soviet Union. Similarly, Britain could not transfer without any loss in efficiency to its prosecution of World War I the resources it used to protect its colonial empire during the late-nineteenth century. Even if the military sector were the sole beneficiary of state j's gains from trade then, w_{ij} would still be less than 1.

When the returns from trade are adjusted to reflect the trading states' marginal social costs, the net effect is to make tariff games between adversaries more difficult to solve than is the standard optimal tariff game. If the game is infinite, free trade can be sustained in an optimal tariff game between adversaries if:

$$(R_i - w_{ij}R_j) / (1 - \delta_i) \geq T_i - w_{ij}S_j + \delta_i(P_i - w_{ij}P_j) / (1 - \delta_i)$$

or

$$\delta_i^* \geq \frac{T_i - w_{ij}S_j - (R_i - w_{ij}R_j)}{T_i - w_{ij}S_j - (P_i - w_{ij}P_j)} \tag{3.2}$$

This condition is more difficult to satisfy than is the condition that emerges from the standard optimal tariff game. In a PD game with payoffs of (3, 2, 1, 0), for example, the minimum discount factor that would support cooperation in the standard game is .50. In the transformed game (with $w_{ij} = .4$), the analogous figure rises to .75.[43] Thus, the utility functions characteristic of adversarial states make any given PD more "severe" or more difficult to solve. In addition, as w increases, the severity of the game also increases.[44]

[43] This is adapted from Snidal (1991).

[44] The game will remain a PD as long as $0 \leq w < 1$. If w equals 1, the mutual reward and mutual punishment payoffs will both equal 0, and the payoff to unilateral defection will be positive. There will not, as a result, be any incentive to cooperate even if the game is repeated.

State j

	Cooperate	Defect
State i Cooperate	$R_i + w_{ij}R_j, R_j + w_{ji}R_i$	$S_i + w_{ij}T_j, T_j + w_{ji}S_i$
Defect	$T_i + w_{ij}S_j, S_j + w_{ji}T_i$	$P_i + w_{ij}P_j, P_j + w_{ji}P_i$

FIGURE 3.6. The Prisoners' Dilemma: Allies
Note: This payoff matrix omits second-order effects.

TARIFF GAMES BETWEEN ALLIES

The gains of one state impose social costs on another only if the former is an actual or potential threat to the security of the latter. When a state trades with an ally, it realizes both private and social benefits from doing so. In the case of allies, then, the external effect of trade is positive. As in the case of trade between adversaries, a utility-maximizing state will take account not only of private but also social returns in calculating its payoffs from trade with allied states.

The standard matrix does not, therefore, apply to this case, either. The transformed PD matrix is shown in figure 3.6. In each cell, the marginal social benefit a state, i, realizes as a consequence of trade with an ally is represented as a fraction, w_{ij}, of the payoff that accrues to its ally, j.[45] This effectively internalizes the positive security externality associated with free trade between allies. The functional form is based on reasoning analogous to that which applies to the case of trade between adversaries.

The applicable incentive-compatibility constraint then becomes:

$$(R_i + w_{ij}R_j) / (1 - \delta_i) \geq T_i + w_{ij}S_j + \delta_i(P_i + w_{ij}P_j) / (1 - \delta_i)$$

or

$$\delta_i^{**} \geq \frac{T_i + w_{ij}S_j - (R_i + w_{ij}R_j)}{T_i + w_{ij}S_j - (P_i + w_{ij}P_j)} \tag{3.3}$$

[45] If w were to equal 1 in the case of allies, and the condition that $2R \geq T + S$ is maintained, the game would be one in which no state had an incentive to defect from the free-trade equilibrium.

This condition is more easily satisfied than is the condition that emerges from either the standard PD or the transformed game between adversaries. Using the same values assigned in the example above, free trade can be sustained among allies when the discount factor is .13. In addition, if w_{ij} exceeds the larger of $(T - R)/(T - S)$ and $(D - S)/(T - S)$, free trade becomes the dominant strategy equilibrium. Thus, tariff games between allies are easier to solve than are tariff games between actual or potential adversaries.[46]

The Effects of Polarity

While the analysis above suggests that all alliances will influence trade, casual empiricism suggests that this effect has been much stronger after than before 1945. Inspection of the incentive compatibility constraint that applies to the intra-allied tariff game suggests one explanation of this difference.[47] All else being equal, the extent to which allies trade freely with each other depends upon the discount factor, δ. The discount factor is inversely related to the probability, θ, that the game will end.

In the context of this analysis, θ can be interpreted as the risk of exit. This risk is the threat that a member will exit or abandon an existing alliance to join an alternative one. For three reasons, it is higher in multipolar than in bipolar systems.[48] First, while alliances in a bipolar world are the products largely of system structure, alliances in a

---

[46] The use of modified PD supergames is not original to this book. See, for example, Taylor (1976); Grieco (1988, 1990); and Snidal (1991). Powell (1991) assigns a low score to their use, because: (1) the games do not allow explicitly for the use of force; and (2) they do not permit payoffs to change over time.

Powell constructs and analyzes a model which he believes overcomes these problems. His analysis generates a clear and striking result. Whether states trade freely with each other depends on the costs of war. If they are high, states do trade freely; if they are low, they do not.

Powell's effort to build a better mousetrap is not a complete success, however, for two reasons. First, his analysis is knife-edged, in the sense that the gain from unilateral defection in the trade game is sufficient to ensure the victory of the defecting state if war ensues. Second, he assumes that complete information about the net benefits of war is available to states ex ante.

[47] I do not intend to imply that this is the *only* explanation. For other possibilities, see Chapter Six.

[48] Empirical analyses support this assertion. See, for example, Duncan and Siverson (1982).

multipolar system reflect choices among several possible alternatives (G. Snyder 1984, 415). Second, in a bipolar system, realignment is impossible for either pole. Third, each pole in a two-power system bears exclusive responsibility for alliance stability. Neither can expect any other state to prevent the defection of an ally from within its bloc (G. Snyder 1984). In a multipolar system, however, interest in preserving alliance stability can be distributed across more than one pole. As a consequence, alliance stability can become problematic, as each pole seeks to transfer the burden of maintaining the alliance to another.

Because the risk of exit is lower in a bipolar than in a multipolar system, the security externalities of any free-trade agreement are more likely to remain internalized within the alliances of the former than within those of the latter. As a result, allies in a multipolar system tend to assign a higher value to θ. Thus, they will discount the future benefits accruing from open markets among them more heavily than will their bipolar counterparts. In contrast, the greater stability of bipolar coalitions allows the value of future benefits to approximate present benefits more closely. Thus, for any given structure of payoffs, free trade is more likely to emerge within the alliances of a bipolar than of a multipolar system.

Two testable hypotheses emerge from the discussion in this chapter: (1) free trade is more likely within than across alliances; and (2) it is more likely within the alliances of a bipolar than of a multipolar world. The next chapter systematically tests these hypotheses.

Alliances and Trade: An Empirical Analysis

WITH EDWARD D. MANSFIELD

USING DATA DRAWN FROM an eighty-year period beginning in 1905, this chapter tests the impact of alliances on trade. The results of the empirical analysis support the argument advanced in the last chapter. They indicate that alliances have a direct, statistically significant, and large effect on bilateral trade. They also indicate that, on average, alliances exert both quantitatively larger and stronger effects on trade in bipolar than in multipolar systems.

This, however, is getting ahead of the story. In the interest of product differentiation, this chapter first reviews the relatively small number of existing empirical analyses of the relationship between international politics and bilateral trade. This review makes it clear that this book defines politics differently; that it rests on different microfoundations; and that it examines a different sample of states and temporal domain than do previous studies. Along the road to product differentiation, some questions are raised about the measures of conflict employed by and the analytic foundations of the literature reviewed.

The next section of the chapter explains the research design that is the basis of the empirical analysis presented here. Succeeding sections develop and test a model of the effects of alliances on bilateral trade. These results indicate that alliances exert a marked influence on bilateral trade. The last section of this chapter demonstrates that the relationship observed does not depend on whether the trading partners are democracies, members of preferential trading arrangements, or parties to military disputes.

TRADE AND THE FLAG

Empirical analyses of the political determinants of bilateral trade are relatively rare. Those that exist can be divided into two groups: (1) those that examine the effects on bilateral trade of preferential trading

54

arrangements (PTAs), such as the European Economic Community (EEC), the European Free Trade Association (EFTA), and the Council of Mutual Economic Assistance (CMEA); and (2) those that analyze the relationship between inter-state political conflict and bilateral trade.[1]

The results of the first group of studies indicate that PTAs tend to increase trade among their members. PTAs are agreements "under which the tariffs nations apply to each others' products are lower than the rates on goods coming from other countries" (Krugman and Obstfeld 1988, 220). Empirical analyses have concluded that these agreements have promoted trade among member nations, although variations exist with respect to the extent to which they do so (see, e.g., Aitken 1973; Linnemann 1966; Pelzman 1977; Tinbergen 1962). The Central American Common Market (CACM) and the EFTA, for example, have had stronger effects on trade than have the EEC, the Latin American Free Trade Area (LAFTA), or the Andean Pact (Brada and Mendez 1983, 555).

Since these studies have found that PTAs are often important determinants of trade patterns, tests will be conducted in this chapter to determine whether any observed relationship between alliances and trade is due to the effects of PTAs. In contrast to this book, existing studies of PTAs tend to focus on the economic rather than on the political incentives of states to discriminate against one another. In addition, they rarely examine the factors that influence the choice of PTA members. As the previous chapter suggests, however, it seems likely that political-military alliances influence PTA membership.

Another difference between these studies and the analysis here is the temporal domain that is examined. The studies in this group focus exclusively on the post-1945 period. As such, they cannot capture the effects of variations in alliances or of polarity on trade, because little variation exists in the alliance patterns and no variation exists in the number of poles during the period that these studies cover. Because both issues are central to the model developed in Chapter Three, the temporal domain of this study includes most of the twentieth century.

The second group of studies centers on the relationship between bilateral trade and conflict (e.g., Gasiorowski and Polachek 1982; Gasiorowski 1986; Polachek 1978, 1980; Pollins 1989a, 1989b). The

[1] As noted in Chapter Two, there have also been some attempts to test hegemonic stability theory. See, for example, Conybeare (1983); McKeown (1982, 1983, 1991); and Mansfield (forthcoming).

conclusion that emerges from this group of studies is that trade and conflict are inversely related. As was true of the first group, the temporal domain of studies in this group is limited to the post–1945 period. The sample of states they use also differs from that used in this book.

In addition, these studies tap a different dimension of international politics. The measure of conflict they employ is based on the events-data compiled in Edward Azar's Conflict and Peace Data Bank (COP-DAB). COPDAB is a computer-based compilation of daily international and domestic "occurrences between nations which are distinct enough from the constant flow of 'transactions' (trade, mail flow, travel, and so on) to stand out against this background as 'reportable' or 'news-worthy'" (Azar 1980, 146).[2] Although these conflict events-data include the conclusion of "strategic alliances," the latter is only one of fifteen categories of events that are used to construct an aggregate measure of conflict and cooperation (Azar and Sloan 1975, vii). Thus, these studies center on a very different aspect of international politics than the aspect that is the focus of the present analysis.

It should also be noted that analysts have raised concerns about the usefulness of some conflict events-data. For example, Charles D. McClelland orginally compiled the "best known and most widely cited" of the extant events-data sets (Howell 1983, 150), the World Event Interaction Survey (WEIS). Nonetheless, McClelland has expressed reservations about their use for some purposes, because the "collections are extracted from the open records of public affairs." As such, he notes, they inevitably reflect "the softness and inconsistency which are characteristics of the source." The "experience of 15 years of published research on international events," McClelland concludes, "instructs us . . . to judge all the results as questionable. . . . [T]he data are dangerous and require careful handling" (1983, 171).

The analytic foundations of works in this second group and the present study also differ. Some of the studies are based on the argument that higher levels of trade lead to lower levels of conflict.[3] Solomon Wil-

---

[2] Azar provides a complete list of publications and countries covered (1980, 151, 152).

[3] Gasiorowski qualifies this argument. He contends that "costly trade produces an increase in conflict while beneficial trade produces a decline in conflict" (1986, 36). The costs associated with trade, according to Gasiorowski, include the complication of domestic macroeconomic planning and the creation of "serious dependencies that expose countries to embargoes or blockades" (1986, 24). All trade imposes some costs, however, because it induces a reallocation of resources that is costless only if textbook conditions are met. Moreover, it is not clear why countries would engage in trade unless its net returns were positive.

liam Polachek, for example, argues that, because welfare increases monotonically with trade, "country pairs with the most mutual international trade should exhibit the least conflict" (1980, 56).[4]

Despite its face validity, this argument warrants close scrutiny. The claim that more trade leads to less conflict cannot be sustained unconditionally. If a political conflict occurs that is serious enough to disrupt trade, a belligerent will incur sizable trade-related costs only if no close substitutes exist for its intradyadic trade. In other words, as Chapter Three suggests, a disruption of intradyadic trade will inflict large welfare costs only if at least one belligerent is able to affect its terms of trade. Thus, under some conditions, the threat of bilateral trade disruption may have no effect on the incidence of conflict.[5]

As a result, any argument about the effect of trade on conflict necessarily applies only to a subset of dyads. Yet, even members of this subset will not necessarily incur trade-related costs. The costs incident upon a conflict-related trade embargo necessarily take the form of deterioration in a country's terms of trade. An interruption of trade can have this effect only if the two countries had, ex ante, concluded a tacit or explicit free-trade truce that prohibited the exploitation of an asymmetric distribution of market power.[6] Allies are more likely than adversaries to have concluded such truces, which suggests that it is the prior *political* relationship between the members of any given dyad that determines whether a bilateral conflict will inflict trade-related costs.

Brian M. Pollins bases his claim about the relationship between conflict and bilateral trade on different analytic foundations. In two recent studies (1989a; 1989b), he advances and finds empirical support for the hypothesis that "trade follows the flag." Two factors explain this relationship, according to Pollins. One, consumers "may wish to express goodwill or solidarity toward those whom they identify as friends, while shunning or punishing those they perceive as foes" (1989b, 740). Two, importers may favor the products of one country as

[4] This argument is also advanced in Gasiorowski and Polachek (1982).

[5] This is not meant to imply that conflict will inflict no trade-related opportunity costs on the parties to it. The prosecution of any large-scale war typically requires belligerents to reallocate domestic resources. This reallocation will itself change prewar trading patterns. This causal chain differs from that invoked in these studies, however, because it is based on the incidental effects on trade of a wartime reallocation of factors of production rather than on a cutoff of trade between belligerents.

[6] Market power must be distributed asymmetrically if conflict is to affect trade. Otherwise, retaliation would make both belligerents worse off than if neither had imposed trade restrictions.

a way of managing risk, that is, an importer may avoid establishing ties with an adversary nation, knowing that those ties may be ruptured by one government or the other as part of some foreign policy maneuver. Thus, in cases where price and quality are roughly comparable, the buyer could choose a seller from a friendly nation in order to *minimize the possibility of economic disruption.* (1989b, 741, emphasis in original)

Pollins imputes to individual importers a utility function which depends not only on "the quantity of goods purchased," but also on "the general friendliness or hostility of . . . political relationship[s] with individual exporters" (1989a, 469). In his view, these "political factors in the utility function reflect traditional security concerns: the desire to reward friends, punish adversaries, and minimize risk" (1989a, 470).

Importers may well have the preferences Pollins attributes to them. With the exception of the risk element discussed below, two factors suggest that this preference attribution is somewhat arbitrary. First, the survey literature suggests that individuals typically do not know much about foreign policy. In 1986, for example, only one-third of the U.S. population could define NATO (Russett and Starr 1992, 219). Thus, the preference function Pollins imputes to importers does not seem to be well grounded in the relevant literature.

Second, it is conceivable that importers may prefer to discriminate among countries of origin even if their actions have no effect on the target countries. They will be able to reward or injure target countries, however, only if their actions change resource allocations in, or the terms of trade of, the target countries. Although not inconceivable, it seems very unlikely that any individual importer will be large enough to accomplish either objective.

As the quotation above makes clear, Pollins's argument about risk management is that "in cases where price and quality are roughly comparable," importers will buy from more rather than less friendly states in order to avoid the disruption that might ensue in the event of an embargo. If, however, as Pollins asserts, close substitutes for the imported good are available, no embargo would be very effective. As a result, it is unlikely that any would ever be imposed. Importers, in turn, would not have strong incentives to discriminate among their sources of supply, unless switching countries of origin inflicts large adjustment costs on them.

In sum, this brief literature review suggests that previous work in this area is not a substitute for the analysis in this chapter. It makes clear that earlier work uses different definitions and measures of political factors; that it relies on different arguments; and that it examines different time periods and countries.

The Research Design

The hypothesis that trade barriers should be lower between allies than between adversaries seems to be eminently susceptible to an empirical test. All that seems to be required is a systematic comparison of the tariff schedules of a random sample of states before and after the inception of an alliance between them. Such an approach, however, is virtually impossible to implement. This is so partly because there are no reliable data on tariffs and other trade barriers for much of the period analyzed in this study. An abbreviation of the temporal domain analyzed might resolve this problem, but only at a prohibitive cost. For example, the analysis might be restricted to the period after 1945. This restriction would make it impossible to assess the impact of alliances on trade. As noted above, little variation in alliances occurred between 1945 and 1985, and no variation occurred in the number of poles during this period.

Moreover, even if tariff schedules were available, it would not be possible to rely on them as a basis of inference about the relationship between alliances and trade. Before World War I and after World War II, trade agreements typically contained a most-favored-nation (MFN) clause. This clause binds a nation to grant any tariff concession it makes to one country to all countries with which the state has preexisting trade agreements.[7]

If countries adhered, not only in principle but also in practice, to MFN clauses, there would be little reason to expect tariffs to vary between allies and adversaries. Indeed, the only outstanding issue would be whether all states adhered to the extant trade regime.[8] In practice,

[7] In the post-1945 period, trade agreements among the advanced industrialized countries conformed de jure to MFN principles, as was required of GATT members. Thus, to put it more precisely, MFN principles governed the trade regime among countries belonging to GATT.

[8] The most obvious example of a country excluded from the MFN regime was the Soviet Union. Because the U.S.S.R. did not belong to GATT, it was susceptible to tariff discrimination. And, in fact, the United States applied Smoot-Hawley tariffs to Soviet imports long after a series of intra-GATT negotiations had reduced U.S. tariffs applicable to GATT members far below Smoot-Hawley levels (Lavergne 1983). For more discussion, see Chapter Six.

nations conformed much more closely to the letter than to the spirit of the MFN clause. The prohibition against explicit discrimination only led nations to create a variety of more or less ingenious substitutes for overt discrimination.

One fairly common substitute was the increasing specialization of tariff schedules. Gottfried von Haberler observed that

> the general tendency has been . . . for tariff schedules to become more extensive, their classifications more complicated, and their individual items more numerous. [One] reason for the increasing complication of tariff schedules is the effort to evade the Most Favoured Nation Clause. To this end, the specialisation of tariff items is carried so far that a slight difference in quality, if it is found only in goods coming from a certain country or countries, is listed as a separate item. In this way it is possible . . . to reduce the duty on goods coming from one country without also reducing it . . . upon similar goods from other countries. (1933, 339)

The evolution of the German tariff schedule illustrates Haberler's point. In 1870, the German schedule levied duties on 230 different goods; in 1888, the same schedule enumerated 490 products; and in 1902, the German schedule specified tariffs on 1800 products (Haberler 1933, 339n4).

In the pre–1914 world, the manipulation of railroad rates was another way in which some states effected de facto discrimination. The Romanian government, for example, levied rates that depended on whether imports entered the country by land or sea.[9] Russia developed an even more finegrained technique. Its railroad rates varied not only between "sea-borne and land-borne" goods, but also among goods that crossed different land frontiers. Moreover, the czarist regime allegedly used its railroad rates "as a weapon in the [1894] tariff war" it waged with Germany.[10]

The same substitution of covert for explicit cross-national discrimination is evident after 1945. Although the MFN principle formally governs trade between GATT members, cross-national discrimination persists. Indeed, the postwar trade regime institutionalizes discrimination by permitting the formation of customs unions and free trade areas (Finlayson and Zacher 1981, 566–7). Other trade barriers that

[9] The intent and effect of this variation was to penalize Britain, inter alia.

[10] The quotations in this and the preceding sentence are from the Board of Trade, "Memorandum on the 'Most Favoured Nation' Principle," January 1904, Public Record Office (hereafter PRO), Cabinet 37/68, 6, 16.

have become common in recent years (e.g., NTBs, especially voluntary export restraints) also discriminate de facto and sometimes de jure.

Thus, because MFN clauses do not eliminate cross-national discrimination but only divert it to other channels, it would be impossible to assess the impact of alliances on trade barriers on the basis of tariff schedules alone. The varied forms of trade discrimination induced by attempts to evade the MFN clause make highly detailed knowledge of a country's exports across time a prerequisite of any such effort. To determine whether the 1906 German tariff discriminated against British silk, for example, it is not enough to know that Britain exported silk; it is also necessary to know the precise form in which it exported silk, because the 1906 tariff enumerated no less than forty-six different subcategories of silk products.[11]

As a result, it is not possible to test directly the hypothesis about the impact of alliances on trade barriers. However, to the extent that alliance patterns explain tariffs and that tariffs, in turn, explain the volume of trade, tariffs are endogenized. The following analysis, therefore, centers on the influence of alliances on bilateral trade flows.[12]

Ideally, the sample of states used to test this hypothesis would include all major powers and their allies. However, data limitations confine the analysis to trade relations among the United States, Great Britain, France, Italy, Germany, the Soviet Union, and Japan during the period from 1905 to 1985.[13] Although this is clearly a limited sample, these states include most of the major powers in the international system during this period (Levy 1983; Small and Singer 1982). Since it is expected that alliances involving major powers will exert a particularly salient impact on trade, this analysis will offer an important, though tentative, test of the model presented in Chapter Three.

[11] "New German Tariff as Modified by Treaties," 1905, Cd. 2414. The British translation of the German tariff schedule runs to more than 225 pages. Because the translation includes data other than the tariff itself, this exaggerates the length of the schedule, but it appears that the tariff schedule alone would be more than 100 pages long.

[12] Of course, trade barriers and trade flows need not always move in tandem. Tariffs, for example, will not be completely endogenized if demand is infinitely inelastic with respect to price.

In addition, the 1970s witnessed the expansion of both trade barriers and trade flows. However, once other determinants of trade are controlled for, these variables should be inversely related; this approach should therefore provide a useful first cut at the problem.

[13] For the period after World War II, West Germany is analyzed; for the period before 1917, Russia is analyzed. In order to simply the presentation, however, the text refers only to Germany and the Soviet Union.

While this model predicts that all alliances will promote trade among their members, an additional hypothesis that this chapter tests is whether bilateral alliances affect trade flows more strongly than do their multilateral counterparts. Trade divergence explains why the effects of the two alliances types might differ. Suppose, for example, that states A and B have concluded a political-military alliance, as well as a free-trade agreement. Suppose, in addition, that both agreements are then extended to state C. If the original bilateral trade agreement diverted trade away from country C, its replacement would increase C's trade with A and B. All other things being equal, this replacement would also reduce the flow of trade between A and B. Thus, a bilateral alliance might influence trade flows more strongly than would a multilateral alliance.

THE MODEL

This section develops a simple model of the relationship between alliances and bilateral trade. It is clear that any analysis of this sort should incorporate economic, as well as political, determinants of trade. Among economists, gravity models of bilateral trade flows have been widely used (Aitken 1973; Anderson 1979; Deardorff 1984, 503–4; Frankel 1992; Leamer and Stern 1970, 145–70; Linnemann 1966; Pelzman 1977; Tinbergen 1962).

Thus, in order to analyze the economic determinants of bilateral trade, a well-known variant of this model is used here. It includes the gross national product (GNP) and the population of both the importer and the exporter, as well as the geographic distance between the two states. Consistent with previous research based on this model, it is expected that the nominal value of bilateral trade will be directly related to the nominal GNP of both the importer and the exporter, and inversely related to the population of both the importer and exporter and to the geographic distance between them.

In addition to GNP, population, and distance, two variables related to alliances are included in the model. The first indicates whether or not a bilateral alliance exists between the trading partners. The second indicates whether or not a multilateral alliance exists between these states. Finally, because interstate wars are expected to reduce trade among the belligerents, a variable that indicates whether or not the importer and exporter are at war is included.

The model is:

$$\log X_{ij(t)} = \log A + B_1 \log Y_{i(t-1)} + B_2 \log Y_{j(t-1)}$$
$$+ B_3 \log P_{i(t-1)} + B_4 \log P_{j(t-1)}$$
$$+ B_5 \log D_{ij(t-1)} + B_6 \log BA_{ij(t-1)} + B_7 \log MA_{ij(t-1)}$$
$$+ B_8 \log War_{ij(t-1)} + \log z_{ij}, \tag{4.1}$$

where $\log X_{ij(t)}$ is the natural logarithm of the nominal value of exports (expressed in U.S. dollars) by state i to state j in year t;[14] $\log Y_{i(t-1)}$ is the natural logarithm of the nominal GNP (expressed in U.S. dollars) of state i in year $t - 1$;[15] $\log Y_{j(t-1)}$ is the natural logarithm of the nominal GNP (expressed in U.S. dollars) of state j in year $t - 1$; $\log P_{i(t-1)}$ is the natural logarithm of the population of state i in year $t - 1$;[16] $\log P_{j(t-1)}$ is the natural logarithm of the population of state j in year $t - 1$; $\log D_{ij(t-1)}$ is the natural logarithm of the geographic distance between states i and j in year t;[17] $\log BA_{ij(t-1)}$ is a dummy variable that equals 1 if an

[14] For the period from 1938 to 1985, all data on exports are taken from the International Monetary Fund (1950, 1956, 1966, 1976, 1986). For the period from 1905 to 1930, data are taken from Bureau de la Statistique Generale (1923, 236); Cacciapuoti (1928, 87–90); Clarke and Matko (1983, 62–73); Department of Finance (1905; 1920); League of Nations (1926, 218–39; 1933, 328–48); Liesner (1989); Mitchell (1980; 1982; 1983); United States Census Bureau (1915, 330–7, 355–6); and United States Department of Commerce (1914, 7–8; 1921, 5–7, 11–12; 1931, 6–9, 14; 1934). In those cases where exports are not denominated in U.S. dollars, exchange rates are taken from Bidwell (1970), Liesner (1989, 54–55), and United States Treasury Department (1904, 1905, 1912, 1913, 1919, 1920).

It should also be pointed out that in some cases, exports by state i to state j are not available. However, in these cases, it is usually possible to find data on imports by j from i. Thus, imports in j's currency are converted into U.S. dollars and used as measures of exports from i to j. These measures should be adjusted to reflect the fact that the value of imports reported sometimes includes transportation costs. It was not possible to do so, however, because sources do not uniformly report on whether import data are net of transportation costs.

[15] Data on nominal GNP for the period from 1904 to 1929 are taken from Gregory (1982), Liesner (1989), and Mitchell (1980, 1982, 1983). In certain cases, reliable data on Soviet and French GNP are not available. In these cases, GNP is estimated using data in Bairoch (1976), Gregory (1982), and Mitchell (1980). Data on nominal GNP and exchange rates for the period from 1937 to 1984 are taken from the United Nations (1948, 1955, 1965, 1975, 1985). For exchange rate data covering the period prior to 1937, see note 14, above.

[16] All data on national population are taken from the Correlates of War Project (1991). It should be noted that since no data on West German population are available for 1954, data for 1955 are used.

[17] Data on geographical distances are found in Fitzpatrick and Modlin (1986) and

alliance exists between states i and j in year $t - 1$ that is comprised of no members except i and j, and 0 otherwise;[18] log $MA_{ij(t-1)}$ is a dummy variable that equals 1 if an alliance exists between states i and j in year $t - 1$ that includes at least one additional member, and 0 otherwise; log $War_{ij(t-1)}$ is a dummy variable that equals 1 if states i and j are engaged in a war in year $t - 1$, and 0 otherwise;[19] and log z_{ij} is an error term. Note that, in antilogarithmic form, all dummy variables in this model take on values of e (the base of the natural logarithms) and 1; the natural logarithms of these variables, therefore, take on values of 1 and 0. Since it is generally assumed that these variables exert a lagged effect on the value of exports, and to reduce problems of simultaneity,[20] a lag of one year in equation 4.1 is assumed for each variable. The log-

---

United States Hydrographic Office (1912, 1936, 1965, 1989). For each pair of states, the shortest distance between ports or rail centers was used to measure the distance between states i and j.

[18] Throughout this study, Small and Singer's (1969) data on alliances are used. Any defense pact, neutrality or nonaggression pact, or entente that is listed by Small and Singer is coded as an alliance. Because the purpose of Small and Singer's study was to explain war, they excluded all wartime alliances from their data. As they themselves observed, however, if their data are used for other purposes, the list of alliances should be amended correspondingly (Small and Singer 1969, 262).

Thus, also included as allies are any states that fought on the same side of any interstate war, as listed by either Levy (1983) or Small and Singer (1982). For present purposes, this results in the inclusion of one multilateral alliance among Great Britain, France, Japan, and the United States in 1919, when these states participated in the Russian Civil War (Levy 1983).

The Japanese–United States Security Treaty (1951–60) and the subsequent Treaty of Mutual Cooperation and Security between these states (1960–present) are also included. Among other things, these treaties called for the United States to come to the aid of Japan in the event that it was attacked (see Grenville 1974, 270, 286–7). As a result, they served much the same purpose as an alliance.

Appendix A provides a complete list of the alliances that this analysis includes.

[19] In this study, any war that is listed by either Levy (1983) or Small and Singer (1982) is analyzed. It might be expected that wars would exert a contemporaneous, as well as a lagged, effect on trade. Since both of the wars considered in this study were being waged in year t, as well as year $t - 1$, any contemporaneous effect of these wars on trade will be captured by the model. Further, it should be noted that only one war (the Changkufeng War (1938)) would be added to the list of wars if this variable was measured in year t, rather than year $t - 1$.

[20] While this strategy reduces potential problems of simultaneity, it is, of course, possible that the relationship between trade and alliances is multidirectional. Although it would also be useful to assess the effect of trade on alliance patterns, developing an adequate model of alliances is beyond the scope of this book.

linear specification of this model is used because it is consistent with many previous studies of trade based on gravity models and because it has a number of advantages relative to a linear specification (Leamer and Stern 1970).

Because the model developed in Chapter Three applies to the relationship between alliances and trade at given points in time as well as over time, equation 4.1 is estimated for a series of cross sections, beginning in 1905. The analysis begins with 1905 (year t), because complete data for all of the independent variables in equation 4.1 are not available prior to 1904 (year $t - 1$). After 1905, the parameters in equation 4.1 are estimated for the first year of each subsequent ten-year interval. However, the model is not estimated during World Wars I and II, since complete trade data are not available for these years. Further, equation 4.1 is not estimated during the late 1940s, because the occupation of Germany and Japan precluded both states from making autonomous decisions about trade policies or alliance partners. As a result, there are some cases in which the intervals are not ten years in length.

Estimates of the Parameters

Ordinary least-squares estimates of the parameters in equation 4.1 are presented in tables 4.1 and 4.2. In each regression, at least one outlier was identified.[21] Since it is useful to determine the extent to which these outliers influence the parameter estimates, the results in table 4.1 are estimated without outliers and the results in table 4.2 are estimated with outliers.

These findings are relatively insensitive to whether or not the outliers are included.[22] On average, the model explains about 80 percent of the variation in the value of exports when the outliers are excluded (in table 4.1) and about 75 percent of the variation in the value of exports when the outliers are included (in table 4.2). The overall fit of the model does not differ substantially across the nine years analyzed.

---

[21] Outliers were identified based on the value of studentized residuals (see Fox 1991, 25–29; Maddala 1988, 412–7).

[22] In regression analyses of this sort, it is important to ensure that the errors are not heteroskedastic. The results of White tests yielded no evidence of heteroskedasticity for any of the estimates reported in this chapter. For descriptions of this test, see Maddala (1988, 162–3) and White (1980).

TABLE 4.1

Regression of Exports on GNP, Population, Distance, Alliances, and War, with Outliers Excluded, 1905–1985[a]

	. . . . . Period of Multipolarity				
	1905	1913	1920	1930	1938
Parameter					
Intercept	−4.57	−8.79	57.21***	7.39	12.44*
	(−.58)	(−.88)	(3.88)	(1.46)	(2.01)
log GNP$_i$	.95***	1.68***	2.78***	1.53***	1.67***
	(5.56)	(7.29)	(8.23)	(11.14)	(8.34)
log GNP$_j$	1.10***	.90***	2.17***	1.25***	1.57***
	(6.15)	(3.55)	(7.91)	(8.79)	(7.20)
log Population$_i$	−.02	−.95***	−4.10***	−1.21***	−1.68***
	(−.06)	(−2.68)	(−4.94)	(−5.22)	(−4.97)
log Population$_j$	−1.21***	−.92***	−4.83***	−1.74***	−2.27***
	(−4.41)	(−2.95)	(−8.13)	(−7.56)	(−6.99)
log Distance$_{ij}$	−.33***	−.06	.27	−.35***	−.06
	(−3.72)	(−.59)	(2.15)	(−5.62)	(−.68)
log Bilateral	−.37	−.57	.20	1.04***	−.30
Alliance$_{ij}$	(−1.18)	(−1.58)	(.26)	(2.46)	(−.75)
log Multilateral	−.61	−.31	.96***	—[b]	.48*
Alliance$_{ij}$	(−1.10)	(−.43)	(2.49)		(1.37)
log War$_{ij}$	−7.12***	—[c]	1.55	—[c]	—[c]
	(−11.68)		(2.15)		
Adjusted R²	.92	.71	.83	.86	.80
N[d]	39	39	37[e]	40	37[f]

[a]Entries are unstandardized regression coefficients with *t*-statistics in parentheses. Years shown are year *t* in equation 4.1.

[b]No multilateral alliances existed among the major powers in 1929.

[c]No wars between major powers were conducted during these years.

[d]For each year, there are forty-two observations minus the number of outliers.

[e]No data on the Soviet Union's exports to Germany are available for 1920.

TABLE 4.1 (continued)

	.... Period of Bipolarity			
	1955	1965	1975	1985
Parameter				
Intercept	34.81***	5.69	6.29	12.14**
	(4.25)	(1.10)	(1.48)	(2.49)
log GNP$_i$	1.12***	.28	.83***	.96***
	(4.31)	(1.07)	(4.06)	(2.98)
log GNP$_j$	.93***	.44**	.55***	.19***
	(3.69)	(1.72)	(2.68)	(3.67)
log Population$_i$	−1.88***	.14	−.68***	−1.13***
	(−3.84)	(.36)	(−2.62)	(−2.71)
log Population$_j$	−1.82***	−.38	−.45**	−1.42***
	(−3.69)	(−.97)	(−1.79)	(−3.51)
log Distance$_{ij}$	−.01	−.12**	−.23***	−.28***
	(−.11)	(−2.10)	(−4.80)	(−3.75)
log Bilateral	3.02***	2.58***	2.07***	2.10***
Alliance$_{ij}$	(5.47)	(6.55)	(6.40)	(4.87)
log Multilateral	.86**	1.65***	.99***	.84***
Alliance$_{ij}$	(1.85)	(5.03)	(5.38)	(3.28)
log War$_{ij}$	—[c]	—[c]	—[c]	—[c]
Adjusted R^2	.78	.82	.82	.80
N[d]	41	40	41	41

[r]No data on Italian exports to the Soviet Union are available for 1938.

*For all variables except the intercept, the regression coefficient has the expected sign and is statistically significant at the .10 level (one-tailed test). For the intercept, the estimate is significant at the .10 level, using a two-tailed test.

**The regression coefficient is statistically significant at the .05 level. See note *.

***The regression coefficient is statistically significant at the .01 level. See note *.

TABLE 4.2
Regression of Exports on GNP, Population, Distance, Alliances, and War, with Outliers Included, 1905–1985[a]

Parameter	..... Period of Multipolarity						..... Period of Bipolarity			
	1905	1913	1920[a]	1930	1938[e]	1955	1965	1975	1985	
Intercept	−3.62	−3.35	51.29**	5.80	14.10	46.90***	15.48***	10.49**	17.15***	
	(−.39)	(−.27)	(2.68)	(.93)	(1.41)	(4.18)	(2.84)	(2.36)	(3.34)	
log GNP$_i$	1.17***	2.07***	2.84***	1.44***	1.78***	.78**	.11	.91***	1.11***	
	(5.25)	(6.54)	(6.83)	(8.41)	(5.96)	(2.19)	(.38)	(4.01)	(3.13)	
log GNP$_j$	1.10***	1.19***	2.42***	1.30***	1.80***	.92***	.26	.45**	.99***	
	(4.93)	(3.75)	(6.08)	(7.61)	(6.01)	(2.57)	(.85)	(1.99)	(2.79)	
log Population$_i$	−.31	−1.82***	−4.18***	−1.14***	−2.16***	−1.76***	.10	−.87***	−1.44***	
	(−.86)	(−4.13)	(−4.50)	(−3.93)	(−4.60)	(−2.53)	(.22)	(−3.11)	(−3.20)	
log Population$_j$	−1.26***	−1.25***	−4.82***	−1.68***	−2.38***	−2.15***	−.40	−.45*	−1.31***	
	(−3.44)	(−2.84)	(−5.78)	(−5.81)	(−4.93)	(−3.10)	(−.84)	(−1.60)	(−2.91)	
log Distance$_{ij}$	−.29***	−.06	.23	−.29***	.07	−.01	−.13**	−.24***	−.27***	
	(−2.63)	(−.44)	(1.32)	(−3.86)	(.58)	(−.08)	(−1.82)	(−4.35)	(−3.32)	
log Bilateral Alliance$_{ij}$	.08	−.26	.07	.99**	−.76	3.52***	2.96***	2.21***	2.29***	
	(.22)	(−.53)	(.06)	(1.85)	(−1.30)	(4.56)	(6.46)	(6.25)	(4.83)	
log Multilateral Alliance$_{ij}$	−.39	−.12	1.54***	—[b]	.43	1.05*	1.79***	.97***	.83***	
	(−.53)	(−.11)	(2.77)		(.77)	(1.60)	(4.60)	(4.77)	(2.88)	
log War$_{ij}$	−6.65***	—[c]	1.40	—[c]	—[c]	—[c]	—[c]	—[c]	—[c]	
	(−8.18)		(1.63)							
Adjusted R²	.86	.61	.72	.77	.64	.66	.77	.79	.78	

aSee table 4.1, note a. For each year, there are forty-two observations unless otherwise noted (see notes d and e).
bSee table 4.1, note b.   cSee table 4.1, note c.   dSee table 4.1, note d.   eSee table 4.1, note e.   fSee table 4.1, note f.
* See table 4.1, note *.   ** See table 4.1, note **.   *** See table 4.1, note ***.

The results shown in tables 4.1 and 4.2 also indicate that the regression coefficients of GNP, population, geographic distance, and war usually point in the expected directions and are statistically significant, regardless of whether the outliers are included or excluded. First, the results in both tables indicate that the regression coefficient of log Y_i is positive in nine cases and statistically significant in eight instances. Further, the regression coefficient of log Y_j is positive and statistically significant in all nine cases, based on the findings in table 4.1. It is positive in nine cases and statistically significant in eight instances, based on the findings in table 4.2. Second, the results in both tables show that the regression coefficient of log P_i is negative in eight cases and statistically significant in seven instances; and that the regression coefficient of log P_j is negative in nine cases and statistically significant in eight instances. Third, the findings in table 4.1 indicate that the regression coefficient of log D_{ij} is negative in eight cases; the findings in table 4.2 show that this regression coefficient is negative in seven cases. Both tables show that it is statistically significant in five instances. Finally, the regression coefficient of log War_{ij} is negative and statistically significant in one out of two cases, based on the results in tables 4.1 and 4.2.

These findings also confirm the hypothesis that alliances are directly related to the value of exports. Table 4.1 shows that the regression coefficient of log BA_{ij} is positive in six out of nine cases. Table 4.2 shows that this regression coefficient is positive in seven out of nine cases. The results in both tables indicate that it is statistically significant in five instances. In addition, the findings in table 4.1 indicate that the regression coefficient of log MA_{ij} is positive and statistically significant in six out of eight cases. The findings in table 4.2 indicate that this regression coefficient is positive in six cases and statistically significant in five instances. Further, the mean of the nine regression coefficients of log BA_{ij}, based on the results in table 4.1, is about 1.09; and the mean of these regression coefficients, based on the results in table 4.2, is about 1.23. Assuming that these regression coefficients are statistically independent, the standard errors of these means are about .15 and .21, respectively.[23] The mean of the eight regression coefficients of log MA_{ij},

[23] Assuming that this condition obtains, the standard error of the mean ($s(\bar{x})$) of the regression coefficients of log BA_{ij} is estimated by:

$$s(\bar{x}) = \frac{1}{n} \sqrt{\left(\sum_{i=1}^{n} s_i^2 \right)}$$

(a)

based on the results in table 4.1, is about .61; the mean of these regression coefficients, based on the results in table 4.2, is about .76. The standard errors of these means are about .16 and .22, respectively.[24] On average, therefore, the relationships between both bilateral alliances and multilateral alliances, on the one hand, and bilateral trade, on the other, seem to be direct and statistically significant.

Moreover, the quantitative impacts of both bilateral and multilateral alliances on the predicted value of bilateral trade are substantial. Even if the means of the regression coefficients of log BA_{ij} were two standard errors less than their respective values, based on the results in tables 4.1 and 4.2, a change from the absence of a bilateral alliance to the existence of such an alliance would more than double the predicted value of exports.[25] Even if the means of the regression coefficients of log MA_{ij} were two standard errors less than their respective values, based on the findings in tables 4.1 and 4.2, a change from the absence

---

where s_i^2 is the estimated variance of the ith regression coefficient of log BA_{ij} and n is the number of cross sections for which this regression coefficient is estimated.

[24] See note 23.

[25] In antilogarithmic form, equation 4.1 can be expressed as:

$$X_{ij(t)} = A\ Y_{i(t-1)}^{B1}\ Y_{j(t-1)}^{B2}\ P_{i(t-1)}^{B3}\ P_{j(t-1)}^{B4}\ D_{ij(t-1)}^{B5}$$

$$BA_{ij(t-1)}^{B6}\ MA_{ij(t-1)}^{B7}\ War_{ij(t-1)}^{B8}\ z_{ij}, \tag{b}$$

where $BA_{ij(t-1)}$ is a dummy variable that equals e if a bilateral alliance exists between states i and j in year $t - 1$, and 1 otherwise. It is clear that if $BA_{ij(t-1)} = 1$ (and log $BA_{ij(t-1)} = 0$),

$$X_{ij(t)} = A\ Y_{i(t-1)}^{B1}\ Y_{j(t-1)}^{B2}\ P_{i(t-1)}^{B3}\ P_{j(t-1)}^{B4}\ D_{ij(t-1)}^{B5}$$

$$1^{B6}\ MA_{ij(t-1)}^{B7}\ War_{ij(t-1)}^{B8}\ z_{ij}. \tag{c}$$

On the other hand, if $BA_{ij(t-1)} = e$ (and log $BA_{ij(t-1)} = 1$),

$$X_{ij(t)} = A\ Y_{i(t-1)}^{B1}\ Y_{j(t-1)}^{B2}\ P_{i(t-1)}^{B3}\ P_{j(t-1)}^{B4}\ D_{ij(t-1)}^{B5}$$

$$e^{B6}\ MA_{ij(t-1)}^{B7}\ War_{ij(t-1)}^{B8}\ z_{ij}. \tag{d}$$

As a result, the proportional increase in the predicted value of exports by state i if there exists a bilateral alliance between states i and j (rather than no bilateral alliance between them) is equal to e^{B6} minus 1. Since the means of B_6 based on the results in tables 4.1 and 4.2 are about 1.09 and 1.23, respectively, and the corresponding standard errors of these means are about .15 and .21, if the means were two standard errors less than 1.09 and 1.23, they would equal .79 and .81, respectively. And since $e^{.79} = 2.20$ and $e^{.81} = 2.25$, the average effect of the change from the absence of a bilateral alliance between states i and j to the existence of such an alliance is to increase the predicted value of exports from i to j by 120 percent and 125 percent, when the remaining variables in the model are held constant.

of a multilateral alliance to the existence of such an alliance would increase the predicted value of exports by more than one-third.[26]

As the model in Chapter Three predicts, polarity has a pronounced influence on the strength and magnitude of the effect of alliances on trade. Regardless of whether the outliers are included or excluded, the means of the regression coefficients of both log BA_{ij} and log MA_{ij} have been substantially larger during periods of bipolarity than during periods of multipolarity, and the differences between these means are statistically significant.[27] Thus, regardless of the type of alliance that is considered, these results indicate that, on average, the magnitude of the effects of alliances on trade have been considerably more pronounced during bipolar than during multipolar periods.

It was hypothesized earlier in this chapter that bilateral alliances exert larger and stronger effects on bilateral trade flows than do multilateral alliances. When the entire time period is considered, the mean of the regression coefficients of log BA_{ij} exceeds that of log MA_{ij}, based on the results in both tables 4.1 and 4.2. But, in neither case is the difference between these means statistically significant.

When bipolar and multipolar years are examined separately, there is evidence that the effects of alliance type on trade depends in large measure on the number of poles in the system. More precisely, considerable support for this hypothesis exists when bipolar periods are examined. The results in tables 4.1 and 4.2 indicate that during bipolar periods the mean of the regression coefficients of log BA_{ij} is considerably larger than the mean of the regression coefficients of log MA_{ij}, and the difference between these means is statistically significant.[28] No support for this hypothesis exists, however, when multipolar periods are analyzed. In fact, the findings in tables 4.1 and 4.2 indicate that the mean of log MA_{ij} is greater than that of log BA_{ij} during the period prior to World War II, although the difference between these means is not statistically significant.

[26] See note 25. This is the case, since $e^{.29} = 1.34$ and $e^{.32} = 1.38$.

[27] For log BA_{ij}, $t = 6.26$ ($p < .005$), based on the results in table 4.1, and $t = 6.49$ ($p < .005$), based on the results in table 4.2. For log MA_{ij}, $t = 2.34$ ($p < .05$), based on the results in table 4.1, and $t = 1.66$ ($p < .10$), based on the results in table 4.2. Note that because the model in Chapter Three predicts that alliances should have quantitatively larger effects in bipolar than in multipolar systems, one-tailed tests are conducted in all cases.

[28] Based on the results in table 4.1, $t = 4.50$ ($p < .005$); based on the results in table 4.2, $t = 4.30$ ($p < .005$).

71

ROBUSTNESS OF THE RESULTS

In addition to estimating the effects of alliances on trade, it is important to analyze the robustness of the results in tables 4.1 and 4.2. To that end, this section addresses two issues. First, does the composition of the sample of states affect these results? More specifically, does the fact that the Soviet Union is included in the sample enhance the influence of alliances on trade? Second, does the omission of certain variables that might be expected to influence both alliance patterns and trade flows account for the observed relationship between alliances and bilateral commerce?

Estimates of the Parameters Excluding the Soviet Union

It is possible that including the Soviet Union in the sample of states that was analyzed in tables 4.1 and 4.2 may have exaggerated the observed impact of alliances on trade. The Soviet Union had both a command and a relatively autarkic economy during most of the twentieth century. It also concluded few alliances with other major powers after World War I. Thus, the strength of the observed relationship between alliances and trade might be due to the composition of the sample. In order to determine whether this is the case, ordinary least-squares estimates of the parameters in equation 4.1 were obtained for those dyads that did not involve the Soviet Union.

These results (and auxiliary regressions based on these results) indicated that, unlike the earlier findings in this chapter, there was often considerable multicollinearity among $\log Y_i$, $\log Y_j$, $\log P_i$, and $\log P_j$ when dyads involving the Soviet Union were excluded from this analysis. One solution to this type of problem is to combine some of the explanatory variables (Fox 1991, 15–16). Therefore, the focus here is on the effects of the nominal per capita GNP (expressed as Y/P) of both the importer and the exporter, as well as distance and alliances, on nominal exports. This specification of the model is as follows:

$$\log X_{ij(t)} = \log A + B_1 \log (Y/P)_{i(t-1)} + B_2 \log (Y/P)_{j(t-1)}$$
$$+ B_3 \log D_{ij(t-1)} + B_4 \log BA_{ij(t-1)}$$
$$+ B_5 \log MA_{ij(t-1)} + \log z_{ij}, \qquad (4.2)$$

where $\log (Y/P)_{i(t-1)}$ is the natural logarithm of the nominal per capita GNP of state i in year $t - 1$; $\log (Y/P)_{j(t-1)}$ is the natural logarithm of the nominal per capita GNP of state j in year $t - 1$; and the nominal per capita GNP of both states i and j is expected to be directly related to the nominal value of exports from i to j (Frankel 1992; Linnemann 1966). Since each of the wars considered in the earlier analysis involved the Soviet Union, War_{ij} is not included in this model. Further, because all alliances in 1929 involved the Soviet Union, it was not possible to estimate the effects of alliances on trade for this year.

Ordinary least-squares estimates of the parameters of equation 4.2 are presented in tables 4.3 (with outliers deleted) and 4.4 (with outliers included). These results indicate that, on average, the model continues to explain about 80 percent of the variation in exports when outliers are included; it explains about 70 percent of the variation in exports when outliers are excluded. Moreover, the signs of the regression coefficients of per capita GNP and geographic distance are in the expected directions. The findings in both tables 4.3 and 4.4 show that, in every case, the regression coefficients of log $(Y/P)_i$ and log $(Y/P)_j$ are positive and statistically significant. Further, the regression coefficient of log D_{ij} is negative and statistically significant in seven out of eight instances, based on the results in table 4.3. It is negative in eight cases and statistically significant in six instances, based on the results in table 4.4.

Of particular interest is the fact that the effects of both bilateral and multilateral alliances on bilateral trade are much the same, regardless of whether the Soviet Union is excluded from the sample of states. In only one case (log MA_{ij} in 1938 in tables 4.2 and 4.4) does the sign of the regression coefficient of either log BA_{ij} or log MA_{ij} change when the Soviet Union is deleted from the sample. In only one case (log MA_{ij} in 1938 in tables 4.1 and 4.3), does the statistical significance of the regression coefficient of either log BA_{ij} or log MA_{ij}, in tables 4.1 and 4.2, change when the composition of the sample is altered. Moreover, the means of the regression coefficients of both log BA_{ij} (1.09 and 1.11, respectively) and log MA_{ij} (.58 and .65, respectively), based on the results in tables 4.3 and 4.4, are quite similar to those based on the results in tables 4.1 and 4.2.

On average, therefore, the relationships between both bilateral and multilateral alliances and bilateral trade continue to be direct and statistically significant. It should also be noted that, on average, the magnitude of the effects of bilateral alliances on trade continues to be significantly larger than that of multilateral alliances during periods of bipolarity (but not during periods of multipolarity); and that, on average, the magnitude of the effects of both bilateral and multilateral al-

TABLE 4.3

Regression of Exports on Per Capita GNP, Distance, and Alliances, Excluding the Soviet Union, with Outliers Excluded, 1905–1985[a]

Parameter	. . . . Period of Multipolarity				. . . . Period of Bipolarity			
	1905	1913	1920	1938	1955	1965	1975	1985
Intercept	9.57***	3.60	2.68	3.17	10.51***	8.73**	8.33***	7.78*
	(3.77)	(1.04)	(.91)	(1.04)	(5.68)	(2.51)	(2.99)	(1.82)
log Per Capita GNP$_i$	1.12***	1.76***	1.88***	1.41***	.80***	.79***	.90***	.69**
	(4.92)	(5.91)	(6.40)	(5.45)	(3.84)	(2.58)	(4.22)	(2.31)
log Per Capita GNP$_j$	.96***	.69***	.94***	1.36***	.51***	.82***	.78***	1.15***
	(4.20)	(2.13)	(3.38)	(5.26)	(2.53)	(2.69)	(3.68)	(3.78)
log Distance$_{ij}$	−.26**	.06	−.21**	−.18**	−.14*	−.17*	−.21***	−.32***
	(−2.30)	(.44)	(−2.01)	(−1.80)	(−1.36)	(−1.60)	(−3.40)	(−3.66)
log Bilateral Alliance$_{ij}$	−.41	−.11	.58	−.21	2.36***	2.41***	2.18***	1.92***
	(−1.05)	(−.26)	(.88)	(−.34)	(4.85)	(4.69)	(6.74)	(4.38)
log Multilateral Alliance$_{ij}$	−.61	−.12	1.06***	.33	1.31***	.93*	.97***	.80***
	(−.97)	(−.16)	(3.06)	(.80)	(2.47)	(1.69)	(3.88)	(2.59)
Adjusted R²	.75	.63	.74	.78	.87	.80	.85	.81
N[b]	28	28	28	28	29	30	28	28

[a] Entries are unstandardized regression coefficients with t-statistics in parentheses. Years shown are year t in equation 4.2.

[b] For each year, there are thirty observations minus the number of outliers.

* See table 4.1, note *.

** See table 4.1, note **.

*** See table 4.1, note ***.

TABLE 4.4
Regression of Exports on Per Capita GNP, Distance, and Alliances, Excluding the Soviet Union, with Outliers Included, 1905–1985[a]

	Period of Multipolarity					Period of Bipolarity		
	1905	1913	1920	1938	1955	1965[b]	1975	1985
Parameter								
Intercept	5.98*	.16	2.99	6.13	12.52***	8.73**	9.73***	9.02*
	(1.84)	(.04)	(.83)	(1.57)	(5.67)	(2.51)	(3.00)	(1.88)
log Per Capita GNP$_i$	1.40***	1.87***	1.87***	1.21***	.60**	.79***	.81***	.69**
	(4.87)	(4.74)	(5.57)	(3.74)	(2.40)	(2.58)	(3.26)	(2.04)
log Per Capita GNP$_j$	1.22***	1.32***	.95***	1.10***	.41*	.82***	.70***	1.00***
	(4.24)	(3.35)	(2.82)	(3.40)	(1.66)	(2.69)	(2.85)	(2.95)
log Distance$_{ij}$	-.16	-.02	-.28**	-.19*	-.17*	-.17	-.21***	-.31***
	(-1.14)	(-.11)	(-2.19)	(-1.44)	(-1.33)	(-1.60)	(-2.83)	(-3.08)
log Bilateral Alliance$_{ij}$	.16	-.16	.49	-.66	2.49***	2.41***	2.20***	1.95***
	(.35)	(-.30)	(.61)	(-.82)	(4.13)	(4.69)	(5.95)	(4.02)
log Multilateral Alliance$_{ij}$	-.11	-.04	1.43***	-.15	1.34**	.93*	.98***	.79*
	(-.13)	(-.04)	(3.51)	(-.29)	(2.04)	(1.69)	(3.50)	(2.38)
Adjusted R²	.68	.57	.69	.62	.79	.80	.81	.77

[a]See table 4.3, note a. For each year, there are thirty observations.
[b]Because no outliers exist, these results are identical to the corresponding results in table 4.3.
* See table 4.1, note *.
** See table 4.1, note **.
*** See table 4.1, note ***.

liances on bilateral trade continues to be significantly larger during bipolar periods than during multipolar periods.

The Effects of Omitted Variables

Another important issue regarding the findings in tables 4.1 and 4.2 is whether these results are robust with respect to the inclusion of variables that are omitted from equation 4.1 and that might account for the observed relationship between alliances and trade. First, as noted above, many analysts have concluded that PTAs have promoted trade among their members. Further, since many of these arrangements have been embedded in alliances, it may be that PTAs are responsible for the observed relationship between alliances and trade.

In order to test this hypothesis, two separate analyses were conducted. Initially, a dummy variable was included in equation 4.1 that equalled 1 if states i and j were members of the EEC in year $t - 1$, and 0 otherwise. Next, a dummy variable was included in equation 4.1 that equalled 1 if states i and j were members of the GATT in year $t - 1$, and 0 otherwise. In each case, 1965, 1975, and 1985 were examined, and both analyses yielded quite similar findings.[29] In each analysis, the regression coefficient of the dummy variable was positive in all three cases (that is, more trade has been conducted between states that were PTA members than between states that were not). But, in each case, only one regression coefficient was statistically significant; and the inclusion of this variable did not have a substantial effect on either the size or level of statistical significance of any of the remaining regression coefficients in equation 4.1.

Second, in addition to wars, military disputes that do not escalate into wars may also influence bilateral trade relations. Further, the existence of military disputes may influence alliance patterns. In order to test whether military disputes account for the observed relationship between alliances and trade, a dummy variable was included in equation 4.1 that equalled 1 if states i and j were involved in a military dispute in year $t - 1$, and 0 otherwise. Among the years listed in tables 4.1 and 4.2, four were marked by military disputes, based on data developed by Gochman and Maoz (1984) and recently updated by the Correlates of

[29] For two reasons, the effects of GATT in 1955 are not examined: (1) all of the states in the sample that were GATT members in 1954 (year $t - 1$) were also NATO members; and (2) for balance-of-payments reasons, several European members of GATT had imposed quotas on imports from the dollar area.

War Project. Analyses of the effects of militarized interstate disputes on bilateral trade indicated that the regression coefficient of this variable tended to be negative (that is, the existence of a dispute involving states i and j tended to depress trade between them); but in no case was it statistically significant.[30] Nor did its inclusion in equation 4.1 substantially change either the size or the level of statistical significance of any of the remaining regression coefficients in the model.

Third, whether or not the states in the sample are democratic polities may account for the observed relationship between alliances and bilateral trade flows. Because their domestic markets are relatively free of government regulations, for example, democracies might trade more with each other than do either nondemocracies with democracies or nondemocracies with each other. Recent research also suggests that democracies have exhibited a disproportionate tendency to ally with one another during portions of the twentieth century (Siverson and Emmons 1991).

In order to determine whether the observed relationship between alliances and trade is due to regime type, a dummy variable was included in equation 4.1 which equalled 1 if both states i and j were democracies in year $t - 1$, and 0 otherwise, based on Doyle's (1986) data. The results indicated that the sign of this regression coefficient varied substantially from year to year and that it was statistically significant in only one case. Moreover, the size and level of statistical significance of the remaining regression coefficients in equation 4.1 continued to be much the same as in tables 4.1 and 4.2.

Clearly, this is not meant to suggest that PTAs, military disputes, and regime type do not influence bilateral trade flows at all. But these factors do not seem to account for the observed relationship between alliances and trade among major powers during the twentieth century. Nor does the composition of the sample: The findings are quite robust with respect to whether or not the Soviet Union is included in the analysis. Thus, the results suggest that bilateral trade flows between major powers tend to be considerably higher when they are allies than when they are not.

[30] While this finding seems to be at odds with the results of the empirical studies reviewed in the first section of this chapter, it is important to note that these studies measure a much wider range of conflictual and cooperative events than those which involve the use of military force. As such, it is difficult to determine the extent to which the apparent weakness of the relationship between militarized disputes and bilateral trade bears on studies that focus on the effects of conflict and cooperation on trade.

Conclusion

The results of the empirical analysis in this chapter suggest that the volume of aggregate trade *is* greater when states are allied with each other than when they are not. The results also make clear that the impact of alliances on trade varies across different international systems. In the preceding chapter, this variation was explained on the basis of differences in the exit risks that prevail in bipolar and multipolar systems.

But exit risk is not the only source of cross-alliance variation: The analysis in this chapter shows that cross-alliance variation also exists *within* international systems. Discussion of potential sources of this variation is deferred until Chapter Six, in order to incorporate the findings contained in the next chapter. That chapter, a case study of the impact of the Anglo-French Entente on British trade policy, is firmly grounded in the real world of trade policymaking. As such, it allows a much richer explanation of the observed variation than would otherwise be possible.

The Anglo-French Entente

THIS CHAPTER is a case study of the Anglo-French Entente.[1] As I noted in Chapter One, the principal reason I chose to examine this case is that the Entente existed during a period of time that deviated from the norm. According to the results of the empirical analysis recorded in the preceding chapter, alliances in the decade before World War I did *not* exert a statistically significant effect on bilateral trade.

The results in Chapter Four do not necessarily apply to all alliances that existed in the pre-1914 decade. Cross-sectional analyses assess the relationship between specified variables in a relatively large number of cases at the same point in time. As a result, it is always possible that the relationship between variables that prevails in any single case is misspecified. Analysis of the Entente demonstrates, however, that the results of the aggregate data analysis apply not only to alliances in general but also to the Anglo-French case in particular. As such, the analysis allows me to speculate about why the pre-1914 period deviated from the norm. Thus, the case study provides a concrete foundation for the more abstract discussion of cross-alliance variation that is the focus of Chapter Six.

Another, decidedly less important, reason why I examine the Anglo-French case is to establish whether hegemonic stability theory miscasts Britain. Although the theory assigns it the role of co-star, Britain has not been subjected to the same kind of scrutiny as has its hegemonic successor.[2] Thus, in this chapter, I attempt to determine whether the principles that governed British trade policy at the turn of

[1] The dating of the Entente in this chapter conforms to that used by Small and Singer (1969) (i.e., the Entente begins in 1904 and ends in 1914, when the advent of World War I led to a multilateral alliance that supplanted the bilateral accord).

[2] In the case of Britain, some variant of endogenous tariff theory seems to have dominated debates about its trade policy. In the case of the United States, debates have more often been driven by Third-Image variables. There are, of course, exceptions to both generalizations. For the British case, see McKeown (1982, 1983) and Stein (1984); for the U.S. case, see Goldstein (forthcoming).

the century conform to those that are the cornerstone of hegemonic theory.[3]

In order to analyze the case, I examined a wide variety of primary and secondary sources.[4] Doing so provided conclusive evidence that the Anglo-French Entente did not affect British trade policy. There is no evidence in British Cabinet records, in the private papers of the three relevant prime ministers, in the records of the Foreign Office, in British tariff schedules, or in other documents suggesting that the Entente exerted any impact whatsoever on British decisions about trade.[5] The documents also suggest that early twentieth-century Britain was a rather ordinary country. Britain was neither a zealous adherent of laissez-faire at home nor a missionary intent upon exporting laissez-faire abroad.[6]

The analytic framework I use in this chapter is based on the model presented in Chapter Three. Thus, I examine the impact (or, more precisely, the apparent absence of such) on British decision-making of: (1) the importance Britain assigned to France (i.e., w_{BF}); (2) the benefits to Britain (i.e., R_B) and the security externality that would accrue to it (i.e., $w_{BF}R_F$) as a consequence of any Anglo-French trade accord; (3) the market power of Britain in the first decade of the twentieth century; and (4) the multipolarity of the pre-1914 world. First, however, I explain why it is impossible to infer the impact of the Entente from tariff schedules alone even in the case of Britain, the alleged exemplar of free trade.

[3] Because they disagree about how to define a hegemon, analysts disagree about the duration of British hegemony. In this study, I follow Krasner, who argues that Britain "was the world's most important trading state from the period after the Napoleonic Wars until 1913" (1976, 375). (Krasner does add, however, that British power peaked about 1880.) Albeit for different reasons, Kindleberger agrees that Britain remained a hegemon until the outbreak of World War I (1973, 28). For dissenting views, see Keohane (1984, 35) and Gilpin (1975, 88–89).

[4] For a complete list of primary sources, see the Primary Sources Reference.

[5] The only possible exception to this statement (Britain's withdrawal from the Brussels Sugar Convention) is discussed in detail later in this chapter.

[6] McKeown (1982, 1984) and Stein (1984) also conclude that Britain was less devoted to practicing free trade at home and exporting it abroad than hegemonic theory suggests. (The reference to Britain as an "ordinary" country is drawn from Rosecrance's characterization of the United States as the latter began its own hegemonic decline [1976].)

BRITISH TARIFF SCHEDULES

As noted in Chapter Four, analyzing the impact of alliances on trade policy seems to require nothing other than a comparison of the relevant tariff schedules before and after the inception of an alliance. This method is more appealing in principle than in practice, for two reasons. Many tariff schedules are simply not available, and those that are available often are impenetrable as a result of covert efforts to evade MFN obligations.

In the British case, tariff schedules *are* available for every year in which the Entente was in effect, as well as for earlier and later years. As a result, it is possible to infer from the schedules alone that the Entente did not influence British trade policy. A comparison of the schedules across time shows that only minor changes occurred in them during the decade of the Entente's existence.[7] Moreover, to the extent that an analysis of the schedules supports Britain's reputation as an exemplar of free trade and a committed adherent to nondiscrimination, the schedules should be both necessary and sufficient to explain the absence of a relationship between the Entente and British trade policy.

Compared to those of other countries at the same time, early twentieth-century British tariff schedules are models of simplicity. It is also true, however, that Britain enumerated and levied duties in a way that conformed to the practice of other countries at that time. It imposed tariffs that were protective and discriminatory in both intent and effect. Thus, had British officials wanted to do so, they could have adjusted import levies to favor France. As a consequence, British tariff schedules are necessary but not sufficient to explain this decision.

Reproduced in Appendix B, the British schedule in effect from March 31, 1910, to March 31, 1911, for example, levied ninety-four separate duties. Among these are tariffs on "Spirits and Strong Waters." Imports in this category were subject to duties that varied as a function of the nineteen different classes into which British officials subdivided them. In a different class, wine imports were subject to duties that increased as a function of the alcoholic strength of the imported wines. British duties on wine also varied according to the form in which it was imported: Higher levies were applied to wine imported in bottles than to imports in casks.

---

[7] It is possible that Britain used NTBs to favor France when the Entente was in effect. There is no evidence in either primary or secondary sources that it did so, however.

Imports of sugar confronted a tariff schedule that was as complex as that applied to alcoholic beverages. Britain levied twenty-four different duties on sugar imports. The degree of "polarization" of the imports— that is, the extent of their refinement—determined the applicable tariff.[8] As discussed in more detail later in this chapter, Britain also sometimes imposed countervailing duties on imports of subsidized sugar.

Thus, British tariff schedules are more similar to those of other countries in the early twentieth century than conventional wisdom suggests. Defenders of Britain's squeaky-clean reputation might reply that British trade practices nevertheless differed in kind: Unlike its counterparts abroad, Britain levied only revenue tariffs, that is, tariffs that generated government revenue but that neither protected home industries nor discriminated across countries. On close inspection, however, this claim is difficult to support.

In principle, revenue and protective tariffs differ. The former "impose a uniform tax on the consumption of an item having no domestic substitutes," while the latter "penalize foreign products for the benefit of local industry" (Nye 1991, 35). In practice, this distinction is problematic. As John Nye has argued, defining protective tariffs as limited to those levied only

> on those items also produced in the home country . . . [ignores] the basic economic fact that there are substitutes for virtually everything. Raise the tariffs on wine and people will drink beer; the tariffs on coffee affect the patterns of tea consumption; and the tariffs on sugar affect not only how the tea will be consumed, but also the foods that the tea will be taken with. (1991, 35)

Moreover, in some instances the British deliberately levied protective tariffs. The desire to protect the domestic bottling industry, for example, motivated the distinction between tariffs levied on wine imported in casks and that imported in bottles. The desire to protect domestic industry also motivated British tariffs on sugar. The differentiation of tariffs on sugar imports on the basis of their degree of polarization apparently was intended to protect the British refining industry.[9]

[8] "Second Report of the Commissioners of His Majesty's Customs and Excise (for the Year ended 31st March, 1911)," Cd. 5827, 1911.

[9] The tariff levied on refined sugar was 9 percent per cwt. (that is, by hundredweight, which equalled 112 lbs.). On all unrefined sugar, the tariff was 6.9 percent per cwt. The tariff on unrefined sugar increased as the degree of refinement increased, ranging from 4.1 percent per cwt. to 9.2 percent per cwt. (calculated by Catherine Jane Gowa from the

Britain's alleged revenue tariffs were also discriminatory in both intent and effect. As discussed in more detail below, the wine schedule, for example, effectively discriminated in favor of Spanish and Portuguese and against French wines, partly because of the important role British shippers played in the wine trade of Spain and Portugal (Nye 1991, 36–37). Similarly, the protection of sugar producers in the British West Indies was the effect, and probable cause, of Britain's adherence to the Brussels Sugar Convention.

Thus, there are fewer qualitative distinctions between British trade practices and those of other countries in the late nineteenth and early twentieth centuries than is commonly believed. Britain's "revenue" tariffs protected domestic industry, and, despite de jure adherence to MFN principles, its import duties intentionally and effectively discriminated among imports according to their country of origin.

Thus, it seems clear that British officials in the early twentieth century could have discriminated in favor of France had they chosen to do so. Neither rigid adherence to free trade nor unyielding commitment to MFN principles stood in their way. As a result, while an analysis of British tariff schedules is sufficient to establish that no such discrimination occurred, it does not suffice to explain the decision of British officials to render trade policy immune to the inception of the *Entente Cordiale*. This explanation requires more data than pre- and post-1904 tariff schedules alone can provide.

Logically prior to any discussion of British trade policy with respect to France, however, is a discussion of the Entente itself. This is the subject of the next section.

THE ANGLO-FRENCH ENTENTE

As Chapter Three makes clear, the weight a state assigns to its ally, w_{ij}, affects the prospects of free trade between them. As a result, it is important to assess the extent to which Britain viewed France as vital to its own security during the decade in which the Anglo-French Entente existed. As will become clear from the discussion that follows, w_{BF} in-

---

"Second Report of the Commissioners of His Majesty's Customs and Excise (for the Year ended 31st March, 1911)," 44). In the absence of price data, it is impossible to be certain about the intent and effect of these tariffs with respect to the British refining industry. The case of sugar, and that of wine, are discussed in more detail later in this chapter.

creased over the duration of the Entente. Indeed, the entry of Britain into World War I made it clear that the interests of the two countries regarding the balance of power on the European continent had become indistinguishable.

The specific provisions of the Entente, however, seem to imply that Britain did not regard France as an important ally in the arena of great-power politics. Instead, the opportunity to strike an extra-European colonial bargain between London and Paris seems to have motivated the Entente. The core element of the 1904 agreement was an exchange of rights between the two countries in Egypt and Morocco. As Paul Cambon, the French ambassador to Britain, observed, "we give you Egypt in exchange for Morocco" (cited in Andrew 1971, 11). The Entente also settled several less important disputes between the two colonial powers, involving Newfoundland, Siam, and the New Hebrides.

The specific provisions of the Anglo-French agreement should not obscure the extent to which it was in fact the product of the great-power politics of the period. The Entente was one of several agreements that Britain concluded with either nascent or actual great powers in the early twentieth century. In 1901, it signed the Hay-Pauncefote Treaty with the United States; in 1902, it concluded a military alliance with Japan; and in 1907, it signed a bilateral agreement with Russia. These agreements had a common origin: steadily increasing threats to the security of Britain and its empire. These included an alliance between France and Russia which effectively challenged Britain's power in the Mediterranean; an increase in French pressure on Morocco which might endanger British control of Gibraltar; and an increase in Russia's ability to threaten British control of India. The Boer War only exacerbated the situation. "Never before," as George Monger notes, "had all the Great Powers concentrated their attention so exclusively on imperial expansion, and never before had Britain been confronted with such intensive competition in every part of the world. The foundation upon which the 'pax Britannica' had been built was now destroyed" (1963, 14).

This trend, as British Foreign Secretary Sir Edward Grey would later point out, made it "essential that our foreign policy should be such as to make it quite certain that there are . . . some nations in Europe with whom it becomes inconceivable that we should find ourselves at war."[10]

[10] "Minutes of the 118th Meeting of the Committee on Imperial Defence" (hereafter CID), July 11, 1912, PRO, Cabinet 38/21, 3.

The realization of this goal depended on a reduction of tensions between Britain and one or more members of the set of existing great powers. As a result, Britain initiated efforts that led to agreements with several states, including France.

The most prophetic element of British diplomacy in this period proved to be the failure to conclude a significant agreement with Germany. Although the two countries did sign several agreements, it quickly became evident that none was a precursor to a general Anglo-German accord. The insuperable obstacle to such an accord was its inability to offer significant benefits to Britain or Germany at a price either country considered less than prohibitive. Germany did not have "sufficient incentive to offer Britain increased security against Russia or France over African or Asian issues, nor Britain to pledge herself in Europe" (Dilks 1981, 3).

Although the constituent elements of the *Entente Cordiale* lay at the periphery of great-power politics, the Anglo-French accord quickly moved to its core. Ostensibly to preserve its role in Morocco, Germany precipitated the watershed event: the 1905 Moroccan crisis. Both Britain and, eventually, France interpreted German intervention in Morocco as an attempt to destroy the Entente.[11] As a result, Germany's action had precisely the opposite effect. After the 1905 crisis, as Eyre Crowe, a senior clerk in the British Foreign Office, would later observe, the Anglo-French Entente

> acquired a different significance from that which it had at the moment of its inception. Then there had been but a friendly settlement of particular outstanding differences, giving hope for future harmonious relations . . . ; now there had emerged an element of common resistance to outside dictation and aggression, a unity of special interests tending to develop into active co-operation against a third power. . . . [T]his new feature of the *entente* was the direct effect produced by Germany's effort to break it up.[12]

[11] Grey observed at the time, for example, that the German action seemed intended "to disturb the Anglo-French entente." Sir Edward Grey to Mr. Whitehead, December 20, 1905, Foreign Office [hereafter FO], Morocco 436, no. 330 (Gooch and Temperley, 1927–38, 160–61). (J. B. Whitehead was the counsellor of the British embassy in Berlin at the time.)

[12] "Memorandum by Mr. Eyre Crowe on the Present State of British Relations with France and Germany," January 1, 1907, FO 371/157 (Gooch and Temperley 1927–38, 402). Although a great deal of debate exists about the influence exerted by this now famous memorandum, professional historians concur in its judgment about the effects of the first Moroccan crisis on the Entente.

The Moroccan crisis also established what would become an enduring characteristic of British-French relations in the ensuing decade. France would seek to formalize Britain's commitment to it. Britain would resist, and the two would agree to a compromise that bound them more closely together but did not formally commit either to the defense of the other.

In early 1906, for example, Cambon asked Grey whether Britain would provide "armed assistance" to France in the event of German aggression against it. Because the imminent general election had dispersed the government, Grey told Cambon that he could "only state my personal opinion that if France were to be attacked by Germany in consequence of a question arising out of the Agreement . . . public opinion would be strongly moved in favour of France."[13]

Although Grey refused to tender any explicit commitment to France, he did authorize the continuation of unofficial Anglo-French military talks that had just begun. Cambon, Grey reported, "thought it advisable that unofficial communications between our Admiralty and War Office and the French Naval and Military Attaches should take place." Their ostensible purpose, Grey noted, was to determine a course of action that "might advantageously be taken in case the two countries found themselves in alliance in . . . a war. Some communications had he believed already passed, and might he thought be continued. They did not pledge either Gov[ernmen]t. I did not dissent from this view."[14]

It was only during the second Moroccan crisis that all members of the British Cabinet became aware of these Anglo-French conversations. While they agreed that the talks could continue, they also insisted that it be made clear that the talks did not bind either side. In mid-July 1912, Prime Minister Henry H. Asquith recorded the consensus of the Cabinet on this issue:

it was agreed that, in continuing the communications which have taken place in the past between the French naval and military experts and our own, it should be plainly intimated to the French Government that such communications were not to be taken as prejudicing the freedom of de-

[13] Sir Edward Grey to Sir F. Bertie, January 10, 1906, FO 371/70, no. 22 (Gooch and Temperley 1927–38, 170–71).

[14] Grey to Bertie, January 10, 1906, PRO, FO 371/70, no. 22.

cision of either Government as to whether they should or should not cooperate in the event of war.[15]

The unwillingness of Britain to commit itself formally to France can be attributed in part to what Glenn Snyder has called the "alliance security dilemma," the delicate balance that allies in a multipolar world must strike between the risk of entrapment and that of abandonment. Because an unambiguous commitment threatens to embolden an ally, it risks entrapment, that is, "being dragged into a conflict over an ally's interest that one does not share" (Snyder 1984, 467). A more ambiguous commitment, however, creates a risk of abandonment, a situation in which a state defects to a rival alliance because it fears that its ally will abandon it in the event of a war.

That British officials recognized the twin dangers inherent in alliances is clear. In 1912, Grey, for example, noted the importance of Britain's ties to France and Russia. But, he added, "we wish also to keep our hands free, so that we shall not be dragged into any European quarrel which does not concern us."[16] Sir Francis Bertie, the British ambassador to France, expressed the same concern even more clearly. While a weak commitment might lead the French to lose confidence in Britain, he observed, "at the same time we must not encourage [them] to rely on our material land support to the extent of making them beard the Germans" (cited in Wilson 1985, 46).

The unwillingness of Britain to formalize its commitment to France can also be attributed partly to the balance of power within Britain. During most of the period in which the Entente was in effect, a split existed within the Liberal Cabinet between the Radical and Liberal Imperialist wings of the party. The Radicals

> were opposed to alliances, both in principle and in practice. They were opposed to anything that smacked of militarism or jingoism. They opposed associating with a Russia still too autocratic for their taste. They opposed the concept of a Triple *Entente*. . . . What they wanted was an agreement with Germany *as well as* an agreement with France and an agreement with Russia. (Wilson 1987, 185, emphasis in original)

Although the Radicals could constrain the Foreign Secretary, they could not challenge him directly. Doing so would only bring down the

[15] Asquith to the King, July 13, 1912, PRO, Cabinet 41/38/58.
[16] "Minutes of the 118th Meeting of the CID," 3.

government. Nor could Grey risk a direct challenge to the Radicals. An uneasy truce resulted. Grey "acknowledged that if he pushed for alliances, he might have to go," and the Radical ministers "acknowledged that if they insisted on neutrality he would certainly go" (Wilson 1985, 36). Thus, both the alliance-security dilemma and an uneasy balance of power at home militated against the conclusion of a formal alliance with France.[17]

Perhaps more important than either was the fact that "the arguments for and against alliances," as Keith M. Wilson observes, "were academic in more senses than one. The decision against alliances represented shutting the stable door" after the horse had bolted, however strenuously the Radical ministers tried to hide this from themselves. "That interests determined actions was admitted," even by the most committed Radicals (Wilson 1985, 58).

Among British interests in this period, none was to become more compelling than the need to confront the implications of an Anglo-German conflict of interests that was becoming irreconcilable. As Paul Kennedy has observed,

> what the Germans supporting Tirpitz desired, whether the vaguer "world political freedom" or the more specific security for German commerce in the event of war, they could not have without affecting Britain's existing naval supremacy. What the latter in turn wished to preserve, command of those waters vital for her own safety as a maritime nation, would be impossible if Germany's goal was reached. What one power wanted, the other would never voluntarily concede; security for one meant danger for the other. (1980, 422–3)

German hegemony in Europe would directly threaten British security. It would enable Berlin to outbuild the British navy and to use continental ports to dominate the English Channel and the high seas. As a result, Britain's "naval supremacy and her interest in the balance of power in Europe were inexorably linked" (Steiner 1977, 59). This implied that Britain's security was also inexorably linked to that of France.

Under these conditions, Britain's refusal to convert the Anglo-French Entente into a formal alliance is not a wholly valid indicator of its commitment to France. The form in which the Entente was expressed was much less important than was the fact that Britain's interests com-

---

[17] As Keith Wilson observes, "alliances and conscriptions were both avoided because either would have split the Liberal Cabinet and raised the question of the future of the Liberal Party" (1985, 57).

mitted London to the defense of Paris. Britain's commitment to France, in short, was dictated not only by the formal ties binding them but also by the interests of Britain itself.

This brief review of the Anglo-French Entente suggests that the strength of Britain's commitment to France increased over the decade in which the Entente was in effect. Although originally an exchange of colonial territories, the Entente very quickly began to reflect the more central interests of the two states that were parties to it. The secular trend in w_{BF} was clearly upward, and in the end, the effective weight Britain assigned to France was indisputably high.

That Britain valued its Entente partner is necessary but not sufficient, however, to predict whether the Entente itself was likely to influence British trade policy. As the argument in Chapter Three makes clear, whether any specific alliance will affect trade policy also depends on the gains to each party of a commercial accord, on market power, and on system structure. These issues are explored in succeeding sections of this chapter.

GAINS FROM TRADE

Between 1904 and 1914, the British Cabinet twice considered whether to open commercial negotiations with France. In late 1906, apparently prompted by a letter from the British Chamber of Commerce, Grey asked his Cabinet colleagues to consider whether Britain should initiate trade negotiations with its Entente partner.[18] In early 1909, Cambon, in a letter to Grey, invited Britain to begin commercial negotiations immediately.[19] The outcome was the same in both cases. The Cabinet unequivocally rejected both initiatives.

The results of the 1906 general election undoubtedly influenced the Cabinet's decision-making. That election was widely interpreted as a referendum on, and a resounding reaffirmation of, Britain's commitment to nondiscriminatory free trade.[20] Two other factors related to this commitment also played a role: the relative dearth of bargaining instruments available to Britain and its aversion to reciprocity as an

[18] Grey to Bertie, November 14, 1906, PRO, FO 800/49.

[19] Board of Trade, "Memorandum on Commercial Negotiations with France and Portugal," February 12, 1909, PRO, Cabinet 37/98, no. 29, 1.

[20] As was pointed out earlier, a gap existed between Britain's commitment to nondiscrimination in principle and in practice.

instrument of trade policy. That the Cabinet did not decide on the basis of these factors alone is clear, however. Its contemporaneous decision to authorize commercial negotiations with Portugal provides strong evidence that other, more idiosyncratic factors also affected its decisions about France.

Among these factors was the legacy of the Franco-Prussian War. The 1871 peace treaty bound France to govern its trade according to unconditional most-favored-nation principles. More specifically, it required France to extend to Germany in perpetuity the benefits of any tariff concessions it made to any of its major trading partners. As a result, Germany could free-ride on the efforts of any country that undertook trade negotiations with France after 1871. That country, in turn, would be forced by the Treaty of Frankfurt to play the "sucker's" role. It would pay all the costs but receive only a fraction of the benefits associated with reaching a trade agreement with France.[21]

The implications of the Treaty were clear to British officials. In his first reply to Grey's inquiry about commercial negotiations with France, Bertie urged the Foreign Secretary to remember that the Treaty allowed Germany to "claim for her trade and commerce any advantages conceded to us by France."[22] In a memorandum to the Cabinet, Board of Trade officials also called attention to the Treaty. France, they noted, "is compelled by the Treaty of Frankfurt to accord to Germany as good treatment as she accords to the United Kingdom and certain other important trading countries."[23]

British officials were also aware that they could attempt to privatize the benefits of any Anglo-French trade agreement. The Board of Trade, for example, suggested that Britain seek tariff concessions on products "which are mainly imported into France from the United Kingdom, so that Germany would obtain no considerable advantage from the concessions, if made." Among the candidate products, the Board noted, were

[21] Paul Wonnacott points out in a more general context that the free-rider problem is the "most notable disadvantage of the MFN clause. . . . Once countries are assured that concessions will be extended to their exports, they may be inclined to sit back, let other countries negotiate lower tariffs, and obtain a 'free ride' when these tariff reductions are extended to their exports" (1987, 41.) The "principal supplier" practice of trade negotiations after 1945 is one way countries tried to circumvent this problem.

[22] Bertie to Grey, November 19, 1906, PRO, FO 800/49, 282.

[23] "Memorandum on Commercial Relations with France," June 9, 1908, PRO, Cabinet 37/93, No. 78.

"Sulphate of copper, Tinplate, Tissues of alpaca, llama, [and] vicuna . . . , Tissues of goats' hair, . . . [and] Gauze and crepe of silk."[24]

But Board officials also warned the Cabinet that even this strategy might not succeed. Because the "production of Germany and the United Kingdom are very much akin," they observed, "it becomes a difficult matter to draw up any exhaustive schedule of goods in respect of which French tariff reductions would be to our advantage exclusively."[25] Other British government officials effectively reinforced this point when they reported that German efforts to privatize its gains from negotiations with Russia had proved futile, because it "was impossible for Germany to fix on any large number of articles in which England was not also partially interested."[26]

In these circumstances, it appeared that Britain might be better off if it took a free ride on the negotiating efforts of other countries than if it undertook them itself. Alfred Marshall, perhaps the most prominent British economist of the time, had earlier explained the logic of this position to the British government. Marshall noted:

> nearly everyone who is trying to get any taxes on imports lowered on behalf of his own country is likely to be working for England's good under this [MFN] clause, unless he gives himself a great deal of trouble to avoid it. The few cases in which he takes the trouble are quoted over and over again . . . , while little is heard of the far more numerous cases in which England's masterly policy of quiescence is rewarded by her reaping the fruits of other people's excitements, quarrels, and worries. The clause, in fact, gives England nearly all that one could obtain by interminable tariff wars, and at no cost.[27]

Thus, it seems clear that the Treaty of Frankfurt adversely affected prospects for commercial negotiations between Britain and France. Because of the similarity between British and German exports, it was very unlikely that Britain would be able to privatize the benefits of any Anglo-French trade agreement.[28] Further evidence, albeit indirect, of

[24] "Memorandum on Commerical Relations," 6.

[25] "Memorandum on Commercial Relations," 6.

[26] "Reports on Tariff Wars Between Certain European States," 1904, Cd. 138, xcv. 701.

[27] "Memorandum by Alfred Marshall on Fiscal Policy of International Trade," [1903] 1908, House of Commons, no. 321, cvii. 23. (Reprinted in Marshall 1926, 411.)

[28] A similar problem existed in the case of the United States between the two world wars. Oye notes that, "from the perspective of trading partners, the Hawley-Smoot Tariff

the importance of this factor is the simultaneous decision of the Cabinet to sanction the opening of commercial negotiations with Portugal.

Unlike France, MFN obligations did not bind Portugal. As a result, Lisbon wielded a credible threat to exclude British exports from its markets. Under the provisions of its 1908 commercial treaty with Germany, Portugal reserved the right to increase tariffs on a list of goods that included "a number of articles of interest to British trade." There is "no doubt," the Board of Trade noted, that "the arrangement is intended by Portugal as a veiled threat to impose further disabilities upon British trade in Portugal unless we come to terms with her."[29]

Because no MFN clause restricted Portugal, its threat to discriminate against Britain was credible. Lisbon did not have to resort to covert and potentially ineffective means to do so. It could instead simply levy higher tariffs on British than on German exports. Thus, Britain could not free-ride on Portuguese-German negotiations. It had to negotiate with Portugal if it did not want Lisbon to discriminate against its exports. Moreover, if it did so, it would not assume the sucker's role. Unlike France, Portugal was not bound to extend to other countries any tariff concessions it accorded to Britain.

Although the record of discussions within the British Cabinet about these negotiations is spare, what there is does suggest that members of the Cabinet were aware that any conceivable Anglo-French commercial accord would yield few tangible returns to Britain. In explaining why the Cabinet decided not to open talks with France, Prime Minister Asquith noted that any "readjustment between the two countries would be of infinitesimal value to British trade."[30]

It also seems clear that the gains from trade which France would receive from any commercial accord with Britain would be very small, as would the concomitant security externality Britain would receive. Both in 1906 and in 1909, the primary commercial target of France was the British tariff on wine. As the MFN clause mandated, British wine duties did not formally discriminate among countries of origin. Instead, they were an in-

---

created a public goods problem. Individual reciprocal tariff reductions were impossible under a single list tariff" (1992, 77). As a result, the U.S. tariff reduced, if not eliminated, the incentives of any country to attempt to decrease trade barriers between it and the United States.

[29] "Commercial Relations Between the United Kingdom and Portugal," February 16, 1909, PRO, Cabinet 37/98, No. 39.

[30] Asquith to King, July 22, 1908, PRO, Cabinet 41/31/64.

creasing function of "the degree and proof of spirit . . . [the imports] contained."[31] Thus, Britain applied the following duties to wine:

Wines containing 30 degrees or less of proof
spirits . . . . 1s. 3d. per gallon
Wines containing over 30 and less than 42
degrees of proof spirit . . . . 3s. per gallon
With an additional 3d. per gallon for each degree above 42[32]

This schedule technically conformed to the prohibition against cross-national discrimination. Because the alcoholic strength of wine exports varied across countries, however, so did the burden of the tariff. Over 90 percent of French wine exports, for example, contained less than 23 degrees of proof spirit; most Spanish exports contained between 26 and 29 degrees of proof spirit. Nonetheless, French exports to the British market were subject to the same levy as were those of Spain.[33]

As Board of Trade officials pointed out, the net effect of the wine scale was that the "amount of duty levied per gallon of proof spirit contained in the wines of different origins" varied across countries. The extant scale, they observed, "presses unduly at each of its extremes. The light French wines are taxed too high; and so also are the full-bodied Portuguese wines." The Board calculated the effective duty on wine imports from different countries as follows:

Duty per gallon of proof spirit

On wine from	s.	d.
Spain	5	6
Portugal	8	1
France	6	10
Germany	5	9
Italy	6	6
Australia	5	4

Board officials argued that a "re-adjustment by which these inequities could be remedied might be very useful at the present time in ce-

[31] H. H. Asquith to Grey, December 22, 1907, Cabinet 37/98, 1909, No. 41.

[32] Board of Trade, "Memorandum on Commercial Relations with France," PRO, Cabinet 38/5, 1904, 8.

[33] The structure of the wine scale was the product of an agreement between Britain and Spain, in which Spain granted MFN status to Britain.

menting our relationship with France, and possibly in obtaining some tariff concessions from her."[34]

The British surtax on wine imported in bottles also adversely affected France. Though nominally a revenue tariff, the surtax, as the Board of Trade pointed out, was, in fact, "a protection to our home bottlers." Nevertheless, the Board added, its abolition would not matter much to the domestic industry, because "only wines of certain brands, guaranteeing special quality or vintage, are or will be imported in bottle. The lighter and more ordinary classes . . . will still come over in cask and have to be bottled here . . . on account of the extra cost of freight which would be involved by bottling on the other side."[35]

It was clear that France would be better off if Britain altered its wine scale and eliminated its surtax on bottled wine. That its gain would be sizable and the concomitant security externality large was much less obvious. In 1905, for example, wine accounted for only about 3 percent of French exports to Britain.[36] Moreover, even if Britain had agreed to eliminate *all* tariffs on French imports, the gain to its Entente partner would still be relatively small. In the aggregate, British import levies imposed only about a 4.5 percent ad valorem tariff on French goods.[37]

Factors other than the magnitude of the material gains that would accrue to Britain and France as a result of any commercial agreement between them also contributed to the outcome of the debate within the British government. Cabinet members were aware that any negotiations with France could endanger, rather than enhance, the security of Britain. Because the conclusion of an Anglo-French commercial accord could be interpreted as a signal of increasing intimacy between London and Paris, it could alienate Germany. Asquith's report on the outcome of the Cabinet's discussion reflects this fear. He noted that:

> after a detailed discussion of this matter . . . , it was the opinion of the
> Cabinet that, on the whole, more harm than good to the interests of the

[34] All figures and quotations in this and the preceding paragraphs are from Board of Trade, "Memorandum on Commercial Relations with France," 4, 9, 10.

[35] Board of Trade, "Anglo-French Commercial Relations," PRO, Cabinet 37/93, 1908, 2.

[36] Calculated from *Statistique Generale de la France Annuaire Statistique* 26 (1906), 211.

[37] Board of Trade, "Memorandum on Commercial Relations with France," 2. This, the Board pointed out, "is due almost entirely to our duties on spirits, sugar, and wine, our duty on French brandy representing an average of about 106 per cent. *ad valorem*, on French refined sugar of about 36 1/2 per cent, and on French wines of about 8 per cent."

United Kingdom and of the Empire would result from opening the question with France. . . . [A]ny readjustment between the two countries . . . might excite suspicion and jealousy—especially in Germany.[38]

In any case, the British government decided twice within a single decade that it would not even consider a new trade accord with France. With one exception, there does not seem to be any evidence either in the British archives or in secondary sources that the Entente influenced British policy in any way. The exception is the attempt of Britain to disengage from the Brussels agreement on sugar. Even in this instance, however, it is not at all clear that the Entente exerted anything other than a nominal effect on British policy.

During the latter half of the nineteenth century, European sugar-producing countries became engaged in an expensive and collectively self-defeating effort to subsidize sugar exports. Because it was an importer rather than a producer of sugar, Britain benefited from the sugar war. Yet, it was Britain that threatened to impose a surcharge on sugar imports unless the principal European exporters agreed to eliminate the subsidies (Ebeling 1914, 94).[39]

Partly as a result of the British threat, the continental sugar producers agreed to a truce. The "International Convention Relative to Bounties on Sugar," concluded in 1902, pledged each of the sugar-producing countries party to it to end the export of "bounty-fed" sugar. The signatory states included, among others, France, Germany, and Austria-Hungary. Although Russia had participated in the negotiations that produced the Convention, it did not sign the Convention, and its abstention initially attracted little attention from the signatory states (Ebeling 1914, 97).

Britain's adherence to the Treaty committed it to observe the procedure set forth in Article IV of the treaty: that is, "to impose a special duty on the importation into [its] . . . territories of sugar from those countries which may grant bounties either on production or on expor-

[38] Asquith to the King, July 22, 1908, PRO, Cabinet 41/31/64. Although there is no evidence in available Cabinet records that a Radical–Liberal Imperialist split influenced the course of the discussion, it seems likely that it did so. Cabinet records are very thin on this issue (as is true of the pre-World War I period more generally), but it seems improbable that the Radicals would have supported any initiative that further solidified relations with France.

[39] Matthias Kaelberer translated from the German all paraphrases and quotations from the Ebeling book that appear in this chapter.

tation."[40] As a 1907 memorandum to the Liberal Cabinet pointed out, Britain's interest in the Brussels Convention was

> entirely different from that of the other contracting States. They are all, or mainly so, producers; we in the United Kingdom are consumers only. The bounty system originated and developed from a competition among themselves for our market. They found as the bounties grew in amount that they were a heavy and growing tax upon themselves. . . . [W]e suffered no such inconvenience, but, on the contrary, were the recipients of those bounties.[41]

As this memorandum suggests, it was distributional rather than efficiency effects that had motivated the Balfour government to threaten a sugar surcharge and adhere to the Sugar Convention. As M. Hicks-Beach, Chancellor of the Exchequer at the time, pointed out, those who stood to gain "pecuniarily by a rise in sugar . . . [were] the owners of West Indian and other sugar estates, their bankers and agents, and the sugar brokers."[42] The losers were British consumers of sugar. As a result of its adherence to the Brussels Convention, Britain "at different times by Orders in Council prohibited imports [of sugar] from Russia, Argentine, Denmark, San Domingo and Spain."[43]

The resignation of the Balfour government and the election of a Liberal government in 1906 suggested that Britain's commitment to the sugar treaty would be short-lived. Entering office with a clear electoral mandate to adhere to free trade, the Liberal government almost immediately confronted the sugar issue. In March 1906, Parliament adopted a motion that favored the abrogation of Britain's commitment to abide by the sugar treaty (Chalmin 1984).

That the commitment was not abrogated immediately seems attributable in part to the concern of Ambassador Bertie, Foreign Secretary Grey, and the Foreign Office more generally that the action would disrupt French sugar exports and, as a result, diplomatic relations with Paris.[44] Noting that Clemenceau had "told me that he was very greatly

[40] "International Convention Relative to Bounties on Sugar," Cd. 1535, Treaty Series, No. 7. 1903, 18.

[41] "The Sugar Convention," PRO, Cabinet 37/88, April 1907, 168.

[42] "Correspondence on the Subject of a Countervailing Duty against Sugar Bounties, no. 2, Sir M. Hicks-Beach to Mr. Chamberlain," PRO, Cabinet 37/45, 1897, no. 52, 4.

[43] Sir Edward Grey to British Delegate, International Sugar Commission, FO 3851, January 27, 1912, Asquith Mss., Bodleian Library, 93, 107.

[44] That Britain continued as a party to the Brussels Convention after the Liberal government assumed office is attributable in part to the fact that the Convention itself was modified in response to British demands in 1907. See Chalmin (1984) for details.

preoccupied by the sugar question," Bertie added that the French prime minister had also told him of efforts by Germany and Austria-Hungary to engage France in "an anti-British combination." Although the proposed combination was "ostensibly" based on their common interests in the sugar market, Bertie noted that "in reality" it had a political objective: to detach France from England.[45]

Grey himself expressed his belief that any decision about the Sugar Convention "is a serious matter and may lead to political consequences."[46] "I realise," Grey stated,

> the importance of the Sugar question and the position of France. The fixed point in the matter which I cannot compromise is that this Parliament will not stand a renewal of the Penal Clause [i.e., Article IV] in the Sugar Convention applicable to this country and insists that we must be free of it on the earliest opportunity. . . . [S]o long as this point of view is not compromised I will do my utmost to meet the French view.[47]

The Liberal government adopted a strategy that seemed designed in part to respond to expressed concerns about France. Rather than announce its intention to withdraw from the Sugar Convention, the Liberal government asked the other contracting parties to release Britain from its Article IV obligations. Grey later told a French official that the continued adherence of Britain to the Convention had occurred "in spite of considerable opposition . . . , and although France had not been mentioned in this connection, people in England assumed that she was the only Power whom His Majesty's Government would have gone out of their way to please."[48]

Even this case, however, raises questions about whether France exerted anything other than a nominal impact on British trade policy. In fairly short order, the Liberal government did persuade the other adherents of the Brussels Convention to relieve it of its Article IV obligations. As a result, as of September 8, 1908, Britain could freely import bounty-fed sugar from Russia, even though the latter was not a party to the original Convention.[49] Thus, the only interest Britain appears to

[45] Bertie to Gray, July 7, 1907, Bertie papers, British Museum, 63020, 156–8.
[46] Edward Grey to Campbell-Bannerman, June 10, 1909, Campbell-Bannerman papers, vol. III, 52514.
[47] Grey to Bertie, July 11, 1907, PRO, FO 800/50, 120.
[48] Bourne and Watt, 1987.
[49] *Economist* (November 9, 1907), 1919.

have sacrificed in order to conciliate France was a brief delay in its ability to import subsidized sugar.[50]

Moreover, the diplomatic record itself is not unambiguous with respect to the importance British officials actually attached to French concerns about sugar exports. Although he faithfully reported Clemenceau's position on the issue to Grey, Bertie also expressed skepticism about the French prime minister's implicit threat:

> I think Clemenceau et al. purposely exaggerated the political [effects].
> . . . I do not see why the French Government should be dragged by a Continental Sugar agreement into a political combination of an Anti-English tendency. . . . There would no doubt be irritation about the Sugar Market . . . , but the entente ought to be able to survive such teacup storms.[51]

It appears that most British officials shared Bertie's skepticism not only about the political implications of abrogation or adherence to the Brussels Sugar Convention but also about Anglo-French trade issues more generally. It is true that Cabinet and other officials did observe occasionally that an increase in Anglo-French trade would have positive effects on political relations between the two countries. In 1909, for example, Prime Minister Asquith expressed his belief that the objective of both Britain and France with respect to trade between them should be to reinforce the Entente.[52] Nonetheless, for reasons made clear in the next section of this chapter, British officials tended to regard trade and security as discrete issue areas.

GOVERNMENT INTERVENTION IN TRADE

In the decade before World War I, British officials seem not to have believed that government intervention in trade could be welfare-

[50] Britain did not actually withdraw entirely from the Convention until 1913, following a simultaneous failure of the European beet crop and the concomitant transformation of a nonbinding to a binding constraint on Russian sugar exports.

[51] Bertie to Grey, July 11, 1907, Bertie Mss., British Museum, 60320, 164. Bertie was not completely consistent in his views, however. See, for example, Bertie to Grey, July 9, 1907, Bertie Mss., British Museum, 63020, 156–8.

[52] Asquith to Mons. Cruppi, March 8, 1909, Asquith Mss., Bodleian Library, 22, Folio 191–3.

enhancing. This belief only governed trade among the great powers, of course.[53] In the case of India, for example, "every sort of non-tariff barrier from the most specific to the most nebulous guaranteed that the lion's share of India's manufactured imports would come from Britain" (Milward 1981, 60).[54]

The secular trend in Britain's world-market power in the immediate pre–World War I years explains in part the arm's-length approach of the country to great-power trade. Britain's power to influence world prices peaked in the mid-nineteenth century. Thereafter, the spread of the industrial revolution precipitated a decline in its market power that was clear not only in retrospect but also at the time. Marshall, for example, took note of this development in a 1903 report to the British government.

In his report, Marshall observed that Britain had at one time exported "manufactures made by steam machinery, which was not in general use anywhere else; together with tropical products which she had special facilities for obtaining."[55] But, Marshall added, Britain's monopoly power had since eroded: Britain's "arts and resources of production have become the common property of all countries in the Western

[53] For a very different view, see Offer (1989). He argues that "the adjustment to economic specialization" was "a root cause" of World War I. "For Britain," he contends, "the Edwardian naval race and the Great War that followed formed a crisis of its system of economic specialization and free trade. . . . Markets require a policeman, and the policeman of nineteenth-century free trade was the Royal Navy. When no single power dominates, free trade no longer resembles the perfect competition of Chicago economics, but the armed vigilance of Chicago's gangsters. The growth of competing powers was not merely a challenge to Britain's economy, it was also a serious danger to its national security" (1989, 402).

The dominant interpretation of World War I, however, rests on factors other than free trade, even as it attends to the Anglo-German naval race. Moreover, the logic of Offer's argument is suspect. Although in Chapter Two, I suggest that cooperation within a small group of states is more difficult than many observers assume, it is not impossible. The "k" group argument suggests that "police forces" from more than one country can, in principle, cooperate to preserve free markets abroad.

[54] In general, as Milward points out, in this period, any country "without the political power to prevent it was likely to have the conditions for its imports laid down by direct intervention by the developed countries, for which the immediate excuse was the need to guarantee the flow of interest payments on earlier capital borrowing." Among the countries "who lost complete tariff autonomy for periods in this way" were Turkey, Greece, Bulgaria, Egypt, and China (1981, 62).

For a more detailed discussion of British tactics with respect to "colonies and other native peoples," see O'Brien and Pignam (1992, 103).

[55] "Memorandum on Fiscal Policy," 6.

world, and in some important cases have been developed by others faster than herself." He also noted that Britain's demand for imports had become more inelastic: A rise in Britain's population "has made her demands for many of her imports more urgent than is the demand of any other country for any of her exports."[56]

More recent observers concur in Marshall's judgment. Douglas Irwin, for example, notes that in "terms of optimal policy from a purely national point of view, Britain may have timed things well: trade restraints in the 1820s and 1830s, then gradually freer trade in the 1840s and thereafter as its monopoly position began to erode." The evolution in British trade policy, according to Irwin, reflected the country's decline in world market power. The ability of Britain

> to derive benefits from the tariff, by which Britain in essence imposed a scarcity of manufactured goods on world markets, was limited. As the industrial revolution spread to other countries, a spread accelerated by its tariff, Britain confronted increasing foreign competition, and its position in world trade became vastly different. (1988, 1,160)

The decline in Britain's power to affect its terms of trade necessarily implied a similar decrease in its ability to use trade policy as an instrument of great-power politics. Because it had become one among several countries capable of wielding market power, any attempt to do so could inflict as much injury on Britain as on its would-be target.

That Britain's world-market power had declined does not, of course, mean that its power had vanished. Britain still could use its trade policy to impose adjustment costs on any country that depended heavily on access to its markets. The decline *did* mean, however, that the play of great-power politics in the immediate pre–1914 period had become increasingly invulnerable to the influence of British trade policy. By then, Germany, Britain's most likely target, had accumulated sufficient market power to ensure that any such attempt would be as costly to London as to Berlin. In 1913, Germany supplied 13 percent of world exports and absorbed an equal share of world imports; Britain's shares were 14 percent and 16 percent, respectively (Hardach 1977, 5).

Thus, it is not surprising that a consensus existed among British officials in this period that intervention in trade would not enhance the country's security. Within the government, the prevailing belief was that the navy was not simply Britain's first, but its *only*, line of defense.

---

[56] "Memorandum on Fiscal Policy," 6.

The primacy assigned to military (i.e., naval) power is manifest in both the tasks assigned to and the conclusions reached by several official committees established in the decade before World War I.

The charge of the "Royal Commission on [the] Supply of Food and Raw Material in Time of War," for example, was "to advise whether it is desirable to adopt any measures, in addition to the maintenance of a strong Fleet" in order to ensure the wartime supply of essential British imports.[57] The report the Commission delivered to the government was unambiguous in its conclusion: A war would not affect in any significant way the ability of Britain to import critical supplies.

The members of the Commission argued, in effect, that Britain faced a highly elastic import supply curve. If "any interference with our supplies from any given source" arose, they stated, "we might expect that a considerable share of the grain now sent from other producing countries to destinations other than the United Kingdom would be diverted to this country."[58] Members of the Commission also believed that the price elasticity of Britain's demand for imports was high. As they put it, "considerable scope for economies in consumption" existed.[59]

The Commission's report issued an explicit warning to the government against the use of stockpiles. Their use, the report argued, would impede rather than enhance the ability of private markets to respond to an import shortage: "The knowledge that a national stockpile exists might deter dealers from endeavoring to import the largest quantities possible, which it would otherwise be in their interest to do."[60]

In short, the members of the Royal Commission warmly embraced the principle of laissez-faire. They did not entertain any doubts about the ability of private markets to respond to British needs even in wartime. They concluded that "with a strong fleet we find no reason to fear such an interruption of our supplies as would lead to the starvation of our people, nor do we see any evidence that there is likely to be any serious shortage."[61] The Commission did, however, suggest to the British government that it establish a committee to consider a system of national indemnities for wartime shipping.[62]

[57] "Report of the Royal Commission on Supply of Food and Raw Material in Time of War, Vol. I: The Report," 1905, Cd. 2643, vol. 39, ix.

[58] "Report of the Royal Commission," 8.

[59] "Report of the Royal Commission," 59. Marshall and the members of the Royal Commission obviously did not agree on this issue.

[60] "Report of the Royal Commission," 52.

[61] "Report of the Royal Commission," 35.

[62] "Report of the Royal Commission," 62.

In 1908, the British government did so. It appointed and charged a committee "to consider and report . . . whether it is desirable that the State shall undertake to make good to shipowners and traders losses incurred through the capture of shipping by the enemy in time of war."[63] The members of the shipping committee turned out to be as sanguine as were their counterparts on the commission for food and raw materials.

The shipping committee members, for example, did not believe that there was any "serious danger" that British ships would be withdrawn from trade in the event of war. Instead, they believed that "the rise in freights, the prospect of increased profits, [and] the large demands of the British War Office and Admiralty in the case of any serious war . . . would rapidly compensate for the increased risk and tempt suitable ships to sea again."[64]

In addition, members of the committee believed that private markets would supply insurance against war risk at reasonable rates "if our Navy did not sustain any serious reverse." They added, however, that even if the navy *did* sustain such a reverse, they would not sanction government regulation. If such a reversal occurred, a "National Guarantee of our sea-borne commerce," they argued, would only "hasten the ruin of the Exchequer without averting the ruin of the Nation."[65]

The committee also maintained that only a national indemnity program was even remotely practical.[66] They would not recommend even that, however, because in their view the cost and incidence of any such program made it infeasible. Their report pointed out that

> a National Indemnity would transfer to the taxpayers at large a liability which is now borne by the individuals immediately concerned, subject to their power of subsequently distributing their losses among the general body of consumers through the medium of enhanced freights and prices. The general community, who under any scheme of indemnity would . . . bear directly the losses incurred by shipowners, merchants, and underwriters, would, on the other hand, have no direct share in the increased profits which successful ventures would secure and which are the natural compensation for increased risks.[67]

[63] "Report by the Committee on a National Guarantee for the War Risks of Shipping to the Lords Commissioners of His Majesty's Treasury," 1908, Cd. 4161, vol. 58, 3.

[64] "Report by the Committee," 10–11.

[65] "Report by the Committee," 13.

[66] An insurance plan would require contributions from the industry; an indemnity plan would be financed by the state.

[67] "Report by the Committee," 28.

In addition, the committee's report noted, any indemnity plan would create severe moral-hazard problems. If shipowners were indemnified against any seizure of cargo, for example, they would "naturally prefer to rely on the guarantee of the British Government rather than prosecute their claims, at considerable expense to themselves and with at best complete uncertainty as to the result, before the Prize Courts of the enemy."[68] Along the same lines, the committee pointed out that

> one of the lessons learnt by underwriters during the Russo-Japanese war was that capture by the enemy would be looked upon as a very useful market by owners, and must be guarded against. It was said that if a shipowner wanted to be sure of "making a good thing," the only certainty of it was to incur a total loss; and one witness stated that, in his opinion, an indemnity would act as a stimulus to shipowners "not in the pursuit of carriage, but in the pursuit of captors for their ships."[69]

No form of state intervention in commercial shipping would, the committee concluded, "secure the safe arrival of ships and cargoes. This is the work of the Navy and the Navy alone."[70] As a result, committee members were "unable to recommend the adoption of any form of National Guarantee against the war risks of shipping and maritime trade, except that which is provided by the maintenance of a powerful Navy."[71]

It seems clear that officials in prewar Britain did not believe that any government intervention in trade, apart from a naval blockade of Germany, would increase Britain's ability to prosecute a war successfully. In the event, however, British officials quickly discovered that they could not pursue a laissez-faire policy with respect to trade, and, as World War I progressed, the British government intervened ever more extensively in both domestic and foreign markets.

Intervention in shipping occurred almost immediately, as the government introduced a war-risks insurance plan and requisitioned ships for the transport of troops and supplies (Ashworth 1960, 277). The advent of the war also led to the adoption in 1915 of the McKenna duties, which levied a 33.3 percent tariff on "luxuries" such as automobiles, clocks and watches, and musical instruments (Capie 1983, 40).[72] In

[68] "Report by the Committee," 29.
[69] "Report by the Committee," 30.
[70] "Report by the Committee," 40.
[71] "Report by the Committee," 42.
[72] Although the McKenna duties, named for the Chancellor of the Exchequer at the

1916, Britain created a Food Product Department which was empowered "to compel farmers to change their cropping and to bring about a large increase of the arable area . . . ; and, where there was a lack of necessary supplies, . . . [to undertake] the bulk buying and resale or such things as seeds, fertilizers and farm machinery" (Ashworth 1960, 281).

By the end of the war, as William A. Ashworth notes, the British government was "directly engaged in far more economic activities than ever before. It purchased abroad 85 per cent of all imported foodstuffs and was the sole buyer of many raw materials." It also controlled approximately 250 munitions factories and had assumed "temporary possession of the railways, coal-mines, flour mills and Irish distilleries. Price control spread far and wide, and private dealings in many commodities were permitted only under license" (1960, 282).

That prewar plans were abandoned as the war progressed was the consequence of a failure to anticipate accurately the duration of the war. As Gerd Hardach observed,

> in none of [the belligerent] . . . countries had any realistic plans been made for feeding the army and the civilian population in case of war. . . .
> In Great Britain food supply was primarily an import problem and hence on the rare occasions before 1914 when wartime policy came up for discussion, it was not regarded as a problem at all. For no one doubted either the ability of the navy to keep open Britain's sea routes, or the ability of the export industry to earn the foreign currency necessary to pay for imported food. The mistake shared by all concerned was to assume that the war would be a short one. (1977, 112)

Conclusion

Not until two years after the outbreak of World War I would high-level British officials even consider explicitly whether Britain ought to extend preferential tariff treatment to its allies.[73] Only in 1916, apparently

---

time, were alleged to be revenue duties, "by normal definition and accepted practice the duties must be regarded as protective since there were no parallel excise duties and they lasted long after the war" (Capie 1983, 40).

[73] Even if all available British documents were reviewed, it would be impossible to be absolutely certain about this. The issue arises only once in the primary documents I did survey (i.e., in the 1916 memorandum cited immediately below), and it does not arise at all in any of the secondary sources I used.

in anticipation of the Paris Economic Conference, did H. Llewellyn-Smith, then permanent secretary of the Board of Trade, prepare a memorandum for the Cabinet which addressed the question of whether Britain should promote trade with its allies by according to them preferential tariff treatment.[74]

Neither the memorandum nor the *Entente Cordiale* had any influence on British trade policy. As such, the analysis in this chapter confirms that the aggregate findings of the empirical analysis in Chapter Four do not apply to the Entente, although the case is consistent with the aggregate results for the pre-World War I period. However, an outstanding issue remains. Do the case-study findings support the central argument of this book?

Hegemonic stability theory would answer this question in the negative. It implies that a causal process different from that specified in Chapter Three was at work. What mattered was the two related roles that Britain allegedly played during parts of the nineteenth and twentieth centuries: (1) free-trade exemplar; and (2) predecessor of the United States as benevolent world despot. If Britain did in fact play both roles, there would be no reason to expect any alliance, including the Entente, to influence its trade policy. How could the *Entente Cordiale* lower British trade barriers if none existed?

The case study proves very interesting in this respect. It tarnishes the reputation of Britain as free-trade exemplar and hegemon.[75] It makes clear that Britain had more barriers to trade than conventional wisdom suggests. It also makes clear that some of these barriers were discriminatory not only in effect but also in intent. As a result, the allegedly zealous adherence of Britain to free and nondiscriminatory trade cannot explain the failure of the Anglo-French Entente to influence British trade policy.

The latter is more appropriately attributed to the failure of the Entente to conform to the assumptions of the model specified in Chapter Three. British officials did not believe, for example, that an Anglo-French commercial agreement would return sizable gains to either

[74] H. Llewellyn Smith, "Post-Bellum Tariff Policy and British Commercial Treaties," Asquith Mss., Bodleian Library, 29, folio 219, n.d.

[75] This is not, of course, the first work to suggest that Britain's reputation is less than sterling. See, for example, Nye (1991); McKeown (1982, 1983); and Stein (1984). The aspects of Britain's reputation that these studies impugn vary. For example, Nye argues that Britain's alleged revenue tariffs protected British industry. McKeown and Stein argue, among other things, that Britain did not seek to lower trade barriers elsewhere.

party. Because Britain had relatively few barriers to trade, France would not gain much nor, because of the Treaty of Frankfurt, would Britain. As a result, the security externality that any Anglo-French accord might produce was also destined to be small.

The Anglo-French case also makes clear that the multipolar system of the pre-1914 world played an important role. In general, multipolar systems create alliance-security dilemmas that are more severe than are those that a bipolar system produces. In the case of the Entente, British officials confronted an alliance-security dilemma that they found difficult to resolve. Although they feared that a strong commitment to France might entrap Britain in wars it had no interest in prosecuting, they also feared that a failure to offer such a commitment might lead France to lose confidence in Britain.

British officials were also concerned about the effects on Germany that its actions with respect to France might have. Typically, battle lines in a multipolar world are not as clearly defined as they are in a bipolar world. Because some ambiguity exists about the identity and depth of enmity of the adversary, a free-trade agreement may have an unintended, adverse effect in a world in which several great powers exist. If it triggers an integrative spiral in another alliance, it may generate security *dis*economies. In the case of the Entente, it seems clear that this danger influenced British decisions about whether to open commercial negotiations with France.

In addition, the British case illustrates the problems that a multipolar system creates for any state with respect to alliance cohesion. The distribution of power within alliances in a multipolar world makes this task more difficult than it is in a bipolar world. Thus, even if it had sought to do so, Britain probably could not have overwhelmed French resistance to a free-trade agreement. In the bipolar world that prevailed after 1945, however, the United States had the requisite leverage.

In sum, the analysis in this chapter, as in its predecessor, suggests that the effects of alliances on trade flows can vary. All alliances are not created equal. In the case of the Entente, an Anglo-French commercial accord threatened to impose net costs on Britain, partly because of the increased enmity with Germany that might have resulted from a trade accord with France. In this respect, the case-study findings differ from those posited in Chapter Three. There, I argued that free trade between allies was less likely in a multipolar than in a bipolar system because of different exit risks.

The case of the Anglo-French Entente makes clear that these risks are not the only source of cross-alliance variation. Thus, it suggests one modification of the theoretical analysis in Chapter Three. In the next chapter of this book, I examine this and other sources of cross-alliance variation in a more general context.

Extensions and Qualifications

IN CHAPTER THREE, I constructed a simple model of the relationship between the anarchic international system and prospects for open international markets. Two testable hypotheses emerged from an analysis of that model: (1) free trade is more likely within than across alliances; and (2) alliances are more likely to evolve into free-trade coalitions in a bipolar than in a multipolar system.

In Chapter Four, these two hypotheses were tested using data drawn from a sample of seven countries over an eighty-year period. The results of the aggregate data analysis supported both hypotheses. They also made it clear, however, that more cross-alliance variation existed than Chapter Three predicted: The impact of alliances on trade varied not only across but also within international systems.

In Chapter Five, some sources of this unexpected cross-alliance variation became evident. The case of the Anglo-French Entente demonstrated, for example, that in some instances the private—and, therefore, the social—returns to free trade can be trivial. The gains that would accrue to Britain from any conceivable Anglo-French trade accord were simply too small to induce British officials to incur the transaction costs involved in any attempt to negotiate an agreement.

In this chapter, I analyze the issue of cross-alliance variation in more abstract terms. I examine potential extensions of and qualifications to the basic model that might explain its occurrence. I attend especially carefully to what appears to be the most plausible and potent source of variation: alliance specificity. That is, the payoffs of optimal tariff games seem to be much more alliance-specific than the model presented in Chapter Three implies. I attribute this variation to political-military and economic factors exogenous to that model.

This analysis of different sources of cross-alliance variation enables me to offer some insights into why such a sharp contrast exists between the pre-1914 and post-1945 patterns of intra-alliance and cross-alliance trade. It also suggests an explanation of why high levels of prewar trade among the states that became belligerents in World War I did not deter the outbreak of that war. I examine these issues briefly in the concluding section of this chapter.

Explaining Cross-Alliance Variation

The game-theoretic analysis in Chapter Three makes it clear that tariff games between allies and adversaries differ. In that analysis, however, I allow only the sign of the social returns to trade to vary. In the case of allies, it is positive; in the case of adversaries, it is negative. Based on this construction, the analysis of the model demonstrates that free trade is more likely between allies than between adversaries.[1]

The empirical analysis in Chapter Four, however, makes it apparent that the outcome of trade games can also vary *across* alliances. Inspection of the incentive-compatibility constraint that applies to trade between allies helps explain why this variation occurs. That constraint, equation 3.3, is:

$$(R_i + w_{ij}R_j) / (1 - \delta_i) \geq T_i + w_{ij}S_j + \delta_i(P_i + w_{ij}P_j) / (1 - \delta_i)$$

or

$$\delta_i^{**} \geq \frac{T_i + w_{ij}S_j - (R_i + w_{ij}R_j)}{T_i + w_{ij}S_j - (P_i + w_{ij}P_j)}$$

Even the most cursory inspection of this constraint suggests one potentially powerful source of cross-alliance variation. If the payoffs to games that different allies play vary, cross-alliance incentives to trade freely obviously will also vary. More precisely, these incentives will be directly related to the payoffs to free trade (i.e., R_i and R_j). They will be inversely related to the payoffs from unilateral defection (i.e., T_i) and to mutual defection (i.e., P_i and P_j). In addition, they will be directly related to the value state i assigns to the parameter, w_{ij}.

Political-military and economic factors exogenous to the optimal tariff games modeled in Chapter Three can explain variations in the payoffs across games between different allies. Among these factors are the magnitude of social returns to trade, factor endowments, the ability to exercise market power, and the transaction costs of negotiating a trade accord. These and several other factors are discussed below.

Political-Military Factors

One of the most important sources of alliance-specific payoffs is cross-alliance variation in the marginal social returns that accrue to a state

---

[1] By implication, free trade is also more likely between allies than between neutrals.

when it concludes a free-trade agreement. This return is a fraction, w_{ij}, of the payoff the ally receives. The value of this parameter, w_{ij}, varies directly with the probability of great-power war. It is also directly related to expectations about whether an ally will actually honor its commitment in the event of war[2] and to expectations about the ability of an ally to influence the outcome of any war.

The variables that affect the probability of war are in some dispute among students of international relations. Among those cited are the distribution of power in the international system (Ordeshook, Niou, and Rose 1989; Waltz 1979); the expected net benefits of war (Bueno de Mesquita 1981; Bueno de Mesquita and Lalman 1992; Gilpin 1981); changes in the distribution of power (Organski and Kugler 1980); the balance between offense and defense, as well as beliefs about that balance (J. Snyder 1984; Van Evera 1984); and the existence of incomplete information (Powell 1992).[3]

Despite a lack of consensus about the causes of war, the value assigned to w_{ij} is likely to increase if the probability state i assigns to the outbreak of a great-power war increases. Allies, it seems obvious, became more important as the threat of war increases: It is their resources that may determine whether victory or defeat ensues. Intra-alliance incentives to conclude a free-trade truce will increase accordingly. Events that occurred during the interwar period illustrate this point. In that period, increasing expectations of a great-power war contributed to the resolution of trade and trade-related conflicts that had plagued states that would later become members of the Western alliance during World War II (see, e.g., Oye 1992). Thus, changes in expectations about the probability of war influence the value states assign to the parameter, w_{ij}, and, therefore, the incentives of prospective or actual allies to trade freely with each other.

However, the probability of war is not the exclusive determinant of w_{ij}. The credibility of alliance commitments also influences the value of this parameter. The discussion of alliances in Chapter Three suggests that whether a state will honor its commitment to another state is problematic unless its interests are indistinguishable and its defense is indivisible from those of its ally. To the extent that interests are more congruent and defense less divisible in bipolar than in multipolar systems, commitments are more credible in two-power systems than in

---

[2] I am indebted to Jeffry Frieden for making this point clear.

[3] For a good discussion of the offense-defense issue, see Jervis (1988).

their multipolar counterparts.[4] Thus, all other things equal, the value assigned to w_{ij} and the prospects for intra-alliance free trade will be inversely related to systemic polarity.

In addition, the income elasticity of demand for military spending of an ally influences the value of w_{ij}, as does the distribution of that spending. A direct relationship exists between the elasticity of demand and the value of w_{ij}. All else being equal, the greater the proportion of its gains from trade an ally is willing to expend on its military sector, the higher will be the marginal social returns to its ally of trading freely with it. As I note in Chapter Three, however, the distribution of spending also matters, because military power is only imperfectly fungible. If the increased expenditure of any given state does not have positive spillovers, it will not have any value for its ally.

Other factors can influence w_{ij}. For example, any change in weapons technology or battlefield strategy that renders ex ante coordination of forces either necessary or superfluous will affect w_{ij}. In addition, if economies of scale in production increase and if access to the affected weapons is restricted to allies, the marginal utility of an ally will increase. As a consequence, incentives to trade freely will also increase.

Economic Factors

In addition to political-military factors, the payoffs of trade games will vary across alliances as a consequence of variations in economic factors. According to the tenets of the Heckscher-Ohlin-Samuelson (H-O-S) model of international trade, for example, gains from trade and differences in relative factor endowments are directly related. This model implies, therefore, that allies with very different factor endowments will have stronger incentives to trade freely with each other than will allies with more similar endowments.

For example, suppose that only two factors of production, land and labor, exist. Suppose, in addition, that the ratio of land to labor is very similar in Germany and France but that it is much higher in the United States. The United States is, in other words, relatively well endowed

---

[4] Cutting the other way, however, is the conventional assumption that allies are more important in a multipolar world, because they can more easily affect the balance of power between opposing coalitions. Whether allies are more important in one system than in another, however, depends on the precise distribution of power in each. Under some specifications, allies can determine the balance between blocs as easily in a bipolar as in a multipolar world.

with land; Germany and France are relatively well endowed with labor. The logic of a factor-endowments model of trade predicts that Germany and France will gain more from trade with the United States than from trade with each other. That is, the payoffs to cross-Atlantic trade will be higher than will those that would accrue from opening borders within Europe.

Another source of alliance-specificity with respect to returns from free trade is implicit in assumptions about whether or not scale economies exist. The H-O-S model assumes constant returns to scale (that is, that output increases equiproportionally as all inputs increase). The assumption of other models is that there are increasing returns to scale (that is, that output increases more than equiproportionally as all inputs increase). As a result, in these models even countries with similar factor endowments—and, as a result, minor differences in comparative costs—have incentives to trade with each other. The relatively large amount of intra-industry trade that exists among the advanced industrialized countries is often used to illustrate the effect of scale economies on trade.[5]

Scale economies can induce variations across alliances in the payoffs to optimal tariff games. Suppose, for example, that France were able to realize much greater economies of scale in production if it opened trade with the United States than if it did so with Britain, because the U.S. market is much larger than is that of Britain. Then, the payoff to France of lifting its barriers to cross-Atlantic trade will be higher than if it eliminated its cross-Channel barriers to trade.

In addition, standard trade theory suggests that incentives to trade freely will be inversely related to the market power of a state. As the elasticity of demand for any state's exports and of the supply of its imports increases, the returns to a state of an optimal tariff, T_i, decrease, and its incentives to trade freely increase. Conversely, if a country confronts highly inelastic export demand or import supply curves, its incentives to open its markets to its allies will decrease.

A comparison between the Organization of Petroleum Exporting Countries (OPEC) and Argentina illustrates this point. In the early 1970s,

[5] If an increased ability to exploit economies of scale is the principal reason that trade expands as a result of a trade accord, the signatories will incur adjustment costs that are relatively low compared to those that result from an expansion of trade based on an increased ability to exploit differences in relative factor endowments. This suggests that economies of scale, as well as "embedded liberalism," explain the success of the postwar series of GATT negotiations (Ruggie 1982).

OPEC controlled a relatively large proportion of the world oil market. Restricting oil exports enabled it to improve its terms of trade.[6] In contrast, Argentina had little if any power to affect the world price of its wheat exports, and, therefore, little or no incentive to restrict trade. Thus, with respect to these two exports, OPEC would pay a higher price than would Argentina if it elected unrestricted trade. Differences in market power, then, are another source of observed cross-alliance variation.

Transaction Costs

Alliance-specific gains from trade can also be the product of the variable transaction costs involved in negotiating a free-trade agreement. As I note in Chapter Two, and as successive rounds of GATT negotiations make clear, efforts to open international markets can easily become contentious. This is a consequence partly of the distributional effects, both within and across states, of open markets. As Chapter Two makes clear, in the absence of perfect markets or an effective redistributive mechanism, more liberal trade can make some groups worse off than if borders had remained closed. Thus, intra-national distributional issues can easily stall trade negotiations.

The argument of this book implies that *cross*-national distributional concerns should pose fewer obstacles to the conclusion of an intra-alliance than to a cross-alliance trade accord. The cross-national distribution of gains from trade matters more when the potential signatory states are adversaries than when they are allies. The effect of trade on the balance of power is not at issue in the case of allies. It is very much at issue, though, in the case of adversaries.

In both cases, the transaction costs of reaching a trade agreement remain positive because of the adjustment costs that accompany trade liberalization. These costs can vary across alliances, depending upon, for example, the impact of any agreement on the ratio of intra-industry to inter-industry trade. If this ratio increases, fewer distributional issues will arise, making transaction costs lower. Thus, differences in ex ante estimates of adjustment costs also help explain why the impact of alliances on trade varies.

The cost of monitoring is another type of transaction cost involved in reaching a trade agreement. Any trade accord, for example, is likely

[6] The rise in oil prices induced an increase in energy efficiency and the supply of oil. As a result, the price of oil in real terms was lower in the late 1980s than it was before the early 1970s (Lairson and Skidmore 1993, 215).

to require a solution to a free-rider problem. Whether or not it makes any sense in theory, it seems common in practice for states to seek to exploit the tariff reductions of other states without making correspond-ing reductions of their own. Ex ante, therefore, states will have stronger incentives to conclude trade agreements with their allies, the easier it is for them to prevent free riding ex post. The ease of exclusion depends on the ability of states to discriminate among the exports and imports of different countries, as well as on whether the imposition of sanctions against would-be free riders benefits the sanctioning states.[7]

Monitoring costs, as well as transaction costs more generally, also seem likely to vary as a function of whether an alliance has been given formal institutional expression. As Keohane has argued, the marginal cost of negotiating a free-trade agreement is likely to be lower if formal structures of cooperation have been established than if they have not (1984). Institutions lower several kinds of transaction costs, among them those incurred to establish a negotiating forum, to standardize the negotiation process itself, and to provide information about the be-havior of states to others.

Institutions also reduce transaction costs to the extent that they mit-igate the aversion of states to act in the absence of support from others. As Lisa L. Martin has shown with respect to economic sanctions in general, institutions influence the incidence of international coopera-tion, because they reduce the risk that a state will find itself acting alone when it sanctions another state (1992, 247). Thus, whether or not an alliance has been institutionalized can also be a source of the alliance-specific character of gains from trade.

This discussion makes clear that allowing the value of other param-eters of the original model to vary can explain why alliances do not uniformly affect trade. It also implies that in some cases adversaries may have the same or even stronger incentives to trade with each other than will some allies. The discussion that follows analyzes two impor-tant real-world cases that support and deepen the observations in this section.

PRE-1914 AND POST-1945 PATTERNS

Implicit in the discussion above is an explanation of: (1) the distinctly different relationships that prevailed between alliances and trade be-

---

[7] Chapter Two contains a more detailed discussion of the enforcement problem.

fore World War I and after World War II; and (2) the inability of high levels of cross-alliance trade to deter the outbreak of World War I. Before detailing this explanation, I briefly describe the pre-1914 and post-1945 patterns.

In the decade that preceded the outbreak of World War I, an intra-alliance integrative spiral triggered a cross-alliance insecurity spiral.[8] Neither, however, exerted much, if any, effect upon pre-existing patterns of trade. And, obviously, relatively high levels of cross-alliance trade did not deter the outbreak of World War I. Less obviously, perhaps, it did not seem to be of any relevance whatsoever to those decision-makers who set out on the road to war.[9]

This message comes through in Chapter Five. Despite an integrative intra-alliance spiral, the Anglo-French Entente exerted *no* discernible impact on British trade policy.[10] That this was not the product of a general aversion to discrimination is clear; Britain did use its tariff schedule to effect cross-national discrimination, although it did not do so in order to reward its allies and punish its adversaries. Although Chapter Five does not address this question directly, there does not seem to be any evidence that rewarding allies and punishing adversaries motivated the trade policies of members of the Triple Alliance.

In contrast, political-military alliances and trade were bound together much more tightly after 1945. During the Cold War, the United States discriminated explicitly against Soviet exports. It applied the highest tariffs in its history, the Smoot-Hawley tariffs, to Soviet and almost all East European exports.[11] In addition, the United States established COCOM in 1950 for the express purpose of embargoing exports of strategic goods to Eastern bloc nations.[12]

[8] For a discussion of these spirals, see G. Snyder (1984).

[9] See, for example, Trachtenberg (1991).

[10] Although Chapter Five does not discuss this explicitly, it does not seem that the inception of the Entente affected French trade policy either.

[11] Questions remain about the actual effect of U.S. tariffs on Soviet exports either to the United States or to the world in general. U.S. tariffs generally escalate as the degree of processing escalates. Most Soviet exports, however, consisted of raw materials which were subject to tariffs that were either low or nonexistent. This might support an inference that U.S. tariffs did not, in practice, discriminate against Soviet exports. It can also support a very different inference: that is, the structure of U.S. tariffs may have influenced the composition of Soviet exports. I am indebted to Gene Grossman for making this point clear.

[12] The economic logic that motivated the composition of COCOM lists was not always compelling, however. As Schelling argued long ago, it made more sense to embargo ag-

The Soviet Union also sought to encourage intra-alliance and to discourage cross-alliance trade. The Soviet Union created the Council for Mutual Economic Assistance precisely in order to encourage trade among members of the Eastern bloc. Indeed, some observers argue that the U.S.S.R. subsidized trade with its East European allies in order to secure "unconventional" gains from trade (i.e., "military, political, and economic nonmarket benefits of bilateral agreements") (Marrese and Janous 1983, 384).[13]

Thus, the pre-1914 and post-1945 worlds differed markedly. In the earlier period, the use of trade to influence the play of great-power politics was almost nonexistent. In the later period, the superpowers waged the Cold War not only on political-military but also on economic battlefields. Differences in the distribution of market power and in system structure help to explain why the great powers played very different games before 1914 and after 1945.

As Chapter Three and the discussion above make clear, market power is a prerequisite of any effort to use trade policy as an instrument of great-power politics. Variation on this dimension seems to explain at least some of the contrast between pre-1914 and post-1945 intra-alliance and cross-alliance trading patterns. In the case of the Anglo-French Entente, the constraints on France imposed by the Treaty of Frankfurt, the fear of alienating Germany, and the exigencies of domestic politics all contributed to the decision of the British Cabinet to refuse to open Anglo-French commercial negotiations. Yet, it seems clear that the secular decline in Britain's world-market power also played a significant role. Any attempt to use trade policy to favor France and injure Germany depended on a degree of asymmetry in the distribution of market power that pre-1914 Britain no longer enjoyed.

In the post-World War II world, the distribution of market power was much more skewed. The United States enjoyed an enormous advantage over the Soviet Union. The U.S. share of industrialized countries' exports rose from 26 percent in 1938 to 35 percent in 1952 (Baldwin, 1984, 8). With the consolidation of NATO and the GATT, the asymmetry became even more marked. To some extent, this asymmetry was a product of World War II. As Alan Milward observes,

---

ricultural than other products to the Soviet Union. An embargo of agricultural exports would force the Soviets to divert resources to a relatively inefficient sector of their economy, thereby imposing higher costs on the U.S.S.R. than would an embargo of goods to its relatively more efficient military sector (cited in D. Baldwin 1985, 215–6).

[13] For a dissenting view, see Brada (1985, 80–92).

there was no major industry [in the U.S.S.R.] whose level of output in 1945 was as high as before the German invasion. . . . In that sense the Soviet Union's experience was the opposite of that of the United States. The U.S.A. emerged in 1945 into a world of exhausted nations with its enormously expanded industries working at full capacity and at higher levels of efficiency than ever before, and with its population enjoying a higher standard of living; Russia entered the post-war world after the most appalling population losses with an enormous armaments industry operating only amidst the wreckage of the Five-Year Plans. (1979, 94–5)

Under these conditions, the U.S. decision to apply high tariffs to Soviet imports across the board seems eminently sensible. The United States enjoyed an asymmetrical influence over its terms of trade that it could use to reduce the real income of the Soviet Union while increasing its own. Moreover, to the extent that the United States could persuade its West European allies to follow its lead, it could inflict additional injury on the U.S.S.R.

The greater dispersion of market power before 1914 than after 1945 was accompanied by a similar dispersion of political-military power. Thus, in the pre-1914 world, it would have been difficult for any one country to persuade its allies to coordinate intra-alliance and cross-alliance trade policy. British decision-makers, for example, were well aware that they could influence French trade policy only at the margins, if at all.

In contrast, the bipolar world that emerged after World War II endowed its constituent great powers with much more influence over their respective allies. Unlike Britain before 1914, the United States after 1945 had enough political-military power to organize its allies into a trading bloc and to forbid them to export strategic goods to Soviet bloc countries.[14] The Soviet Union also possessed a significant degree of leverage over its allies.

The bipolar structure of the post-World War II world also made it clear to both the United States and the Soviet Union that no opportunity existed to "pass the buck."[15] If neither acted to secure its alliance bloc, no other country would do so. Thus, any attempt to evade the "buck-

[14] Mastanduno (1988) argues that it was convergent preferences, rather than power disparities, that explain the short-lived willingness of Western Europe to accept the U.S. vision of an export-control program.

[15] See Posen (1984) for a discussion of the buck-passing that occurred in the interwar period.

stopping" role would only render the postwar alliances impotent: neither NATO nor the WTO would be cohesive and powerful enough to act as effective weapons in the waging of the Cold War. Thus, in contrast to the period before World War I and between the two world wars, the distribution of power after 1945 facilitated the formation and institutionalization of political-military alliances that could also be used to coordinate and deploy trade policy effectively as an instrument of power politics.

The dispersion of market power that characterized the pre–1914 world also helps explain why high levels of cross-alliance trade did not deter the outbreak of World War I. If trade is to act as a significant deterrent to war, the opportunity costs of disrupting prewar trading patterns must be high. Large volumes of trade between or among prospective belligerents, however, are not necessarily a valid indicator of the trade-related opportunity costs of war.

Instead, what really matters is whether close substitutes exist for the export markets and imports that prewar trading partners supplied. If such substitutes exist, then the trade-related opportunity costs of war will be low. This is precisely what the dispersion of market power implies: the existence of substitutes for imports and export markets. As the analysis of the British case suggests, the dispersion of market power in the pre–World War I period implied that the trade-related opportunity costs of war would not be very large, despite the high levels of cross-alliance trade.[16]

CONCLUSION

In this chapter, I confront directly an important issue that became apparent earlier: the variable impact of alliances on bilateral trade. I suggest that alliance-specific payoffs play a very important role in explaining this variation. This alliance-specificity is, I contend, a function of both political and economic factors. I then draw on this discussion to explore differences in the pattern of intra-alliance and cross-alliance trade before 1914 and after 1945 and the failure of trade to deter the outbreak of World War I.

The analysis in this chapter makes clear that the model presented in

---

[16] As I note in Chapter Four, this does not, of course, include the trade-related costs that accrue from the reallocation of domestic factors of production incident upon war.

Chapter Three captures an important distinction between intra- and cross-alliance trade. It also makes clear, however, that the real world is much more complex than is the model itself. Although this is true by definition, it does suggest several ways in which the model could be profitably extended. Among them, for example, is making the value assigned to the parameter, w_{ij}, endogenous.

In the next (and last) chapter, I reprise the argument and results of the empirical analyses presented in this book. I also examine their implications for the study of international relations.

Conclusion

DURING THE COLD WAR, it seemed difficult to explain the pattern of global trade without reference to the two major political-military blocs of that period. NATO and GATT were two sides of one coin; the WTO and CMEA were the two sides of another. That political-military alliances strongly influenced international trade seemed not only indisputable but also unproblematic.

Yet, hegemonic stability theory, the most prominent system-level explanation of the political determinants of inter-state trade, remained almost wholly impervious not only to the Cold War that raged around it but also to the logic of political life in an anarchic world more generally. It does not seem to have occurred to Kindleberger, for example, that there might be something problematic about a hegemon's willingness to assume the role of "benevolent [global] despot" (1973).

Most students of international relations believe that unabashedly self-interested states populate the world. In their view, there is no reason to believe that economic issues induce more altruistic behavior from states than do political issues. The analysis of Britain in this book, as well as other studies of both Britain and the United States, offer powerful support for this belief. None suggests that either state subordinated the pursuit of its national interests to global interests during the period in which it reigned as the alleged free-trade hegemon.

Nor would it have made sense for Britain, the United States, or any other state to do so. Because trade produces security externalities, it should not be any less vulnerable to the play of great-power politics than is any other type of state interaction. Trade with an ally produces a positive externality; trade with an adversary creates a security diseconomy. As a result, ceteris paribus, free trade is more likely within than across political-military alliances.

An explicit analysis of the external effects of trade helps explain the strong association between alliances and trade that prevailed during the Cold War. The advent of a bipolar international system induced less fluid alliance patterns and less dispersion of market power than had prevailed earlier. As a consequence, it made the evolution of political-military alliances into free-trade coalitions much more likely.

The aggregate data analysis presented in this book supports the basic argument about the relationship between alliances and trade, as well as the argument about the effect of system structure. The analysis demonstrates that alliances do, indeed, have a direct, statistically significant, and large effect on bilateral trade. It also demonstrates that, on average, alliances in a bipolar world exert more influence on trade than do their counterparts in a multipolar world.

The empirical analysis also suggests that the effect of alliances on trade varies not only across but also *within* international systems. Perhaps most striking was the apparent absence of any relationship between alliances and trade in the pre-1914 period. Because data limitations restrict the temporal domain to one which begins in 1905, it is impossible to know whether this result also applies to earlier periods.

A case study of the Anglo-French Entente suggests several potential sources of the cross-alliance variation that the results of the aggregate data analysis reveal. For example, it makes clear the importance of the magnitude of the expected gains from any trade accord plays. Because the marginal private and social returns that would accrue from any trade agreement were likely to be small, Britain refused to incur the costs that Anglo-French commercial negotiations would impose on it. These and other sources of cross-alliance variation are discussed in detail in Chapter Six; the discussion bears neither repetition nor summary here.

In short, although the analysis here is not exhaustive, it seems clear that an attempt to tie trade to the flag can be a profitable strategy to pursue. Because political-military alliances internalize the external effects of trade, it makes sense for states to trade more freely with allies than with actual or potential adversaries. Caution is clearly indicated, however. As I have argued in this book, and as the literature on economic sanctions more generally makes clear, binding trade to the flag does *not* make sense under all conditions. The ability to exercise market power is the most basic prerequisite of any attempt to bind trade to the flag that does not inflict net costs on the state which does so.

Even with this caveat, argument and evidence presented in this book imply that the division of international relations into two discrete subfields does not make a lot of sense. It can be much more difficult to distinguish the pursuit of power from the pursuit of plenty than this disciplinary divide suggests. Life in an anarchic world demands that states attend not only to the balance of political-military power, but also to other spheres of international interactions, including trade, which can indirectly affect that balance. This, in turn, demands that students of international relations do so as well. Neither students of international security nor those of international political economy can afford to neglect developments in the other subfield. The pursuit of power and of plenty are two sides of the same coin.

Appendix A

LIST OF ALLIANCES

1904

Austria-Hungary–Germany–Italy
Austria-Hungary–Germany–Italy–Romania
France–Russia
France–Italy
England–Japan
England–France

1912

Austria-Hungary–Germany–Italy
Austria-Hungary–Germany–Italy–Romania
France–Russia
France–Italy
England–Japan
England–France
France–Japan
Japan–Russia
England–Russia
Italy–Russia

1919

England–Japan
England–France–Japan–United States

1929

Germany–Russia

1937

France–Russia
Italy–Russia
France–Italy
Germany–Japan–Italy

1954

Belgium–Canada–Denmark–England–France–Iceland–Italy–Luxembourg–
  Netherlands–Portugal–United States–Greece–Turkey
Australia–England–France–New Zealand–Pakistan–Philippines–Thailand–
  United States
Japan–United States

1964

Belgium–Canada–Denmark–England–France–Iceland–Italy–Luxembourg–
  Netherlands–Portugal–United States–Greece–Turkey–West Germany
Australia–England–France–New Zealand–Pakistan–Philippines–Thailand–
  United States
Japan–United States

1974

Belgium–Canada–Denmark–England–France–Iceland–Italy–Luxembourg–
  Netherlands–Portugal–United States–Greece–Turkey–West Germany
Australia–England–France–New Zealand–Pakistan–Philippines–Thailand–
  United States
Japan–United States

1984

Belgium–Canada–Denmark–England–France–Iceland–Italy–Luxembourg–
  Netherlands–Portugal–United States–Greece–Turkey–West Germany
Japan–United States

Source: Levy 1983; Small and Singer 1969, 1982.

BRITISH IMPORT DUTIES, 1910–11

SECOND REPORT

OF THE

COMMISSIONERS OF HIS MAJESTY'S CUSTOMS AND EXCISE.

(For the Year ended 31st March, 1911.)

BEING THE

55TH REPORT RELATING TO THE CUSTOMS

AND THE

54TH REPORT RELATING TO THE EXCISE.

Presented to both Houses of Parliament by Command of His Majesty.

LONDON:
PUBLISHED BY HIS MAJESTY'S STATIONERY OFFICE.
To be purchased, either directly or through any Bookseller, from
WYMAN AND SONS, LTD., FETTER LANE, E.C., and 32, ABINGDON STREET, S.W.; or
OLIVER AND BOYD, TWEEDDALE COURT, EDINBURGH; or
E. PONSONBY, LTD., 116, GRAFTON STREET, DUBLIN.

PRINTED BY
DARLING AND SON, LTD., BACON STREET, E.
1911.

[Cd. 5827.]   *Price* 9½*d.*

15

TABLE 8.—The Customs Tariff of the United Kingdom for 1910-11.
(1.) Import Duties.

Articles.	Rates of Duty.		
	£	s.	d.
Beer of the descriptions called Mum, Spruce, or Black Beer, and Berlin White Beer, and other preparations, whether fermented or not fermented, of a character similar to Mum, Spruce, or Black Beer, where the worts thereof were, before fermentation, of a specific gravity—			
Not exceeding 1215° ... ... for every 36 gallons	1	13	0
Exceeding 1215° ... ... „ „	1	18	8
Beer of any other description where the worts thereof were, before fermentation, of a specific gravity of—			
1055° ... ... for every 36 gallons	0	8	3
(And so on in proportion for any difference in gravity.)			
Cards, Playing ... ... the dozen packs	0	3	9
Chicory :—			
Raw or kiln-dried ... ... the cwt.	0	13	3
Roasted or ground ... ... the lb.	0	0	2
Chloral Hydrate ... ... „	0	1	9
Chloroform ... ... „	0	4	4
Cocoa ... ... „	0	0	1
Husks and shells ... ... the cwt.	0	2	0
Cocoa or Chocolate, ground, prepared, or in any way manufactured ... ... the lb.	0	0	2
Cocoa Butter ... ... „	0	0	1
Coffee ... ... the cwt.	0	14	0
Kiln-dried, roasted or ground ... ... the lb.	0	0	2
Coffee and Chicory (or other vegetable substances), roasted and ground ; mixed ... ... „	0	0	2
Collodion ... ... the gallon	1	14	11
*Confectionery, containing Chocolate :—			
When the Chocolate exceeds 50 per cent. of the total net weight the lb.	0	0	1¾
When the Chocolate does not exceed 50 per cent. of the total net weight ... ... „	0	0	1¼
Ether, Acetic ... ... „	0	2	7
„ Butyric ... ... the gallon	1	1	10
„ Sulphuric ... ... „	1	16	6
Ethyl Bromide ... ... the lb.	0	1	5
„ Chloride ... ... the gallon	1	1	10
„ Iodide ... ... „	0	19	0
Fruit, Dried, or otherwise Preserved without sugar :—			
Currants ... ... the cwt.	0	2	0
Figs and Fig Cake, Plums, commonly called French Plums, and Prunelloes, Plums Dried or Preserved, not otherwise described, Prunes, and Raisins the cwt.	0	7	0
NOTE.—Plums include Greengages, Damsons, Mirabelles, and Dried, Crystallised, or Glacé Apricots. Tinned and Bottled Apricots in Syrup or Water, and Apricot Pulp, are not liable to Duty as Preserved Plums, but when added Sugar is present, as in the case of Syrup, they are chargeable under the heading of Sugar (which see).			
Dutiable Fruit imported in Syrup or Water is to be assessed with duty at 7s. the cwt. on the weight of Fruit without squeezing out the contained Syrup or Water. The Syrup in such cases is separately charged with its proper duty, unless the merchant elects to pay duty on the whole weight at the fruit rate.			
Motor Spirit ... ... the gallon	0	0	3
Subject to repayment if the Spirit is to be used for purposes other than supplying motive power to Motor Cars, or to repayment of 1½d. the gallon when the Spirit is used for supplying motive power to Motor Cars employed for Commercial purposes, &c.			
Glucose, Solid ... ... the cwt.	0	1	2
„ Liquid ... ... „	0	0	10
Molasses and invert Sugar and all other Sugar and extracts from Sugar which cannot be completely tested by the Polariscope and on which duty is not otherwise charged :—			
If containing 70 per cent. or more of sweetening matter ... the cwt.	0	1	2
If containing less than 70 per cent. and more than 50 per cent. of sweetening matter ... ... the cwt.	0	0	10
If containing not more than 50 per cent. of sweetening matter „	0	0	5
Molasses is free of duty when cleared for use by a licensed distiller in the manufacture of Spirits, or if it is to be used solely for purposes of food for stock.			

* An additional ½d. the lb. is chargeable in respect of Chocolate Confectionery in the manufacture of which Spirit has been used. Confectionery in the manufacture of which a greater percentage of Spirit has been used than that covered by the Spirit charge of ½d. the lb. is chargeable with a Spirit duty rate of 1d the lb. or such Spirit duty rate in excess of 1d. the lb. as analysis may show to be necessary.

16

Import Duties—*continued.*

Articles.	Rates of Duty.
	£ s. d.
Saccharin and Mixtures containing Saccharin, or other substances of like nature or use ... ... the oz.	0 0 7

NOTE.—Saccharin and Mixtures containing Saccharin or other substances of like nature or use must not be imported into the United Kingdom in packages containing less than 11 lbs., and must not be packed with goods of any other description, and must be specially reported and imported and entered for Warehousing at the following ports only :—
Dover, Folkestone, Goole, Grangemouth, Grimsby, Harwich, Hull, Leith, London, Newhaven, Southampton, and West Hartlepool.

Soap, Transparent, in the manufacture of which Spirit has been used... the lb.	0 0 3

	Imported in Casks.	Imported in Bottles.
Spirits and Strong Waters :—		
For every gallon computed at hydrometer proof of Spirits of any description (except Perfumed Spirits), including Naphtha or Methylic Alcohol, purified so as to be potable; and mixtures and preparations containing Spirits—	£ s. d.	£ s. d.
Enumerated Spirits :—		
Brandy ... ... the proof gallon	0 15 1	0 16 1
Rum ... ... ,,	0 15 1	0 16 1
Imitation Rum ... ... ,,	0 15 2	0 16 2
Geneva ... ... ,,	0 15 2	0 16 2
Additional in respect of Sugar used in Sweetening any of the above tested for strength, if Sweetened to such an extent that the Spirit thereby ceases to be an Enumerated Spirit ... the proof gallon	0 0 1	0 0 1
Unenumerated Spirits :—		
Sweetened ... ... ,,	0 15 3	0 16 3
(Including Liqueurs, Cordials, Mixtures, and other preparations containing Spirits ; if tested.)		
Not Sweetened ... ... the proof gallon	0 15 2	0 15 2
(Including Liqueurs, Cordials, Mixtures, and other preparations containing Spirits, provided such Spirits can be shown to be both Unenumerated and Not Sweetened ; if tested.)		
Liqueurs, Cordials, Mixtures, and other preparations containing Spirits, not Sweetened, provided such Spirits are not shown to be Unenumerated ; if tested ... ... the proof gallon	0 15 2	0 16 2
Liqueurs, Cordials, Mixtures, and other preparations containing Spirits, in Bottle, entered in such a manner as to indicate that the strength is not to be tested .. .. the liquid gallon	—	1 1 5
Perfumed Spirits ... ... ,,	1 4 1	1 5 1

Any importations of Naphtha or Methylic Alcohol purified so as to be potable are taken under the heading of Unenumerated Spirits.

The *minimum* legal size of packages of Spirits (other than Cordials or Perfumed or Medicinal Spirits and Spirits imported in Cases) is in Casks or other vessels of a size or content of not less than nine gallons.

Upon payment of the difference between the Customs Duty on Foreign Spirits, and the Excise Duty on British Spirits, Foreign Spirits may be delivered under certain conditions for Methylation or for use in Art or Manufacture, but foreign Methylic Alcohol may be used in Art or Manufacture without the payment of this differential duty.

Sugar :—	£ s. d.
Not exceeding 76 degrees of Polarization ... ... the cwt.	0 0 10
Exceeding 76 and not exceeding 77 ... ... ,,	0 0 10·9
,, 77 ,, ,, 78 ... ... ,,	0 0 11·2
,, 78 ,, ,, 79 ... ... ,,	0 0 11·6
,, 79 ,, ,, 80 ... ... ,,	0 0 11·9
,, 80 ,, ,, 81 ... ,,... ... ... ,,	0 1 0·3
,, 81 ,, ,, 82 ... ... ,,	0 1 0·6
,, 82 ,, ,, 83 ... ... ,,	0 1 1
,, 83 ,, ,, 84 ... ... ,,	0 1 1·4
,, 84 ,, ,, 85 ... ... ,,	0 1 1·8
,, 85 ,, ,, 86 ... ... ,,	0 1 2·2
,, 86 ,, ,, 87 ... ... ,,	0 1 2·6
,, 87 ,, ,, 88 ... ... ,,	0 1 3
,, 88 ,, ,, 89 ... ... ,,	0 1 3·4
,, 89 ,, ,, 90 ... ... ,,	0 1 4
,, 90 ,, ,, 91 ... ... ,,	0 1 4·5

For Rates of Duty on Articles made with Sugar *see* Table 55.

17

Import Duties—*continued.*

Articles.		Rates of Duty.		
		£	s.	d.
Sugar—*cont.*				
Exceeding 91 and not exceeding 92 ... ... the cwt.		0	1	5
„ 92 „ „ 93 ... ... „		0	1	5·6
„ 93 „ „ 94 ... ... „		0	1	6·1
„ 94 „ „ 95 ... ... „		0	1	6·6
„ 95 „ „ 96 ... ... „		0	1	7·1
„ 96 „ „ 97 ... ... „		0	1	7·7
„ 97 „ „ 98 .. .. „		0	1	8·2
„ 98 — ... ... „		0	1	10
Tea ... ... the lb.		0	0	5
Tobacco :—				
Manufactured, viz. :—				
Cigars ... ... „		0	7	0
Cavendish or Negrohead ... ... „		0	5	4
Cavendish or Negrohead, Manufactured in Bond ... ... „		0	4	8
Other Manufactured Tobacco, viz. :—				
Cigarettes ... ... „		0	5	8
Other sorts ... ... „		0	4	8
Snuff containing more than 13 lbs. of moisture in every 100 lbs. weight thereof ... ... the lb.		0	4	5
Snuff not containing more than 13 lbs. of moisture in every 100 lbs. weight thereof ... ... the lb.		0	5	4
Unmanufactured, if Stripped or Stemmed :—				
Containing 10 lbs. or more of moisture in every 100 lbs. weight thereof ... ... the lb.		0	3	8½
Containing less than 10 lbs. of moisture in every 100 lbs. weight thereof ... ... the lb.		0	4	1½
Unmanufactured, if Unstripped or Unstemmed :—				
Containing 10 lbs. or more of moisture in every 100 lbs. weight thereof ... ... the lb.		0	3	8
Containing less than 10 lbs. of moisture in every 100 lbs. weight thereof ... ... the lb.		0	4	1
NOTE.—The minimum weight of packages of Tobacco allowed to be imported into the United Kingdom is 80 lbs. gross. Packages of Tobacco must contain Tobacco only, and under Tobacco are included Cigars, Cigarillos, Cigarettes, and Snuff.				
Wine :—				
Not exceeding 30° of Proof Spirit ... ... the gallon		0	1	3
Exceeding 30° but not exceeding 42° of Proof Spirit ... ... „		0	3	0
And for every degree or part of a degree beyond the highest above charged, an additional duty ... ... the gallon		0	0	3
The word "degree" does not include fractions of the next higher degree.				
Wine includes Lees of Wine.				
Additional—				
On Still Wine imported in Bottles ... ... the gallon		0	1	0
On Sparkling Wine imported in Bottles ... ... „		0	2	6
All Wines must be entered according to their commercial designations, those from Spain being also described on the Entry as "Red" or "White."				

Bibliography

PRIMARY SOURCES

Private Papers:

1. Public Record Office, Kew: (Gerald) Balfour, Bertie, Grey, Hardinge, Lansdowne, Nicholson.
2. Bodleian Library, Oxford: Asquith.

Official Papers:

1. Public Record Office, Kew:
   Cabinet and Committee of Imperial Defence series: 37 (the photographic copies of Cabinet papers, 1881–1916); 38 (the photographic copies of minutes and memoranda of the Committee on Imperial Defence, 1888–1914); 41 (Cabinet letters in the Royal Archives, 1868–1916).
2. Parliamentary Papers, London:
   United Kingdom. Parliament. "New German Tariff as Modified by Treaties." Cd. 2414, 1905.
   United Kingdom. Parliament. "International Convention Relative to Bounties on Sugar." Signed at Brussels, March 5, 1902. Treaty Series, no. 7, Cd. 1535, 1902.
   United Kingdom. Parliament. Report by the Committee on a National Guarantee for the War Risks of Shipping to the Lords Commissioners of His Majesty's Treasury. Cd. 4161, 1908.
   United Kingdom. Parliament. Reports of the Commissioners of His Majesty's Customs and Excise (various years).
   United Kingdom. Parliament. Report of the Royal Commission on Supply of Food and Raw Material in Time of War. Cd. 2643, 1905.

SECONDARY SOURCES

Aitken, Norman D. 1973. The Effect of the EEC and EFTA on European Trade: A Temporal and Cross-Section Analysis. *American Economic Review* 63: 881–92.

Altfeld, Michael F. 1984. The Decision to Ally: A Theory and Test. *Western Political Quarterly* 34:523–44.

Anderson, James E. 1979. A Theoretical Foundation for the Gravity Equation. *American Economic Review* 69:106–16.

Andrew, Christopher. 1971. The Entente Cordiale from its Origins to 1914. In

Troubled Neighbors: French–British Relations in the 20th Century, edited by Neville Waites. London: Weidenfeld and Nicolson.

Ashworth, William A. 1960. *An Economic History of England.* London: Methuen.

Axelrod, Robert. 1984. The *Evolution of Cooperation.* New York: Basic Books.

Axelrod, Robert, and Robert O. Keohane. 1985. Achieving Cooperation under Anarchy: Strategies and Institutions. *World Politics* 38:226–54.

Azar, Edward E. 1980. The Conflict and Peace Data Bank (COPDAB) Project. *Journal of Conflict Resolution* 24:143–52.

Azar, Edward, and Thomas J. Sloan. 1975. Dimensions of Interaction. *Occasional Paper No. 8.* University of Pittsburgh Center of International Studies.

Bairoch, Paul. 1976. Europe's Gross National Product, 1800–1985. *Journal of European Economic History* 5:273–340.

Baldwin, David A. 1985. *Economic Statecraft.* Princeton, N.J.: Princeton University Press.

———. 1987. Politics, Exchange and Cooperation. Paper prepared for delivery to the 28th Annual Convention of the International Studies Association, Washington, D.C.

Baldwin, Robert E. 1984. The Changing Nature of U.S. Trade Policy since World War II. In *The Structure and Evolution of U.S. Trade Policy,* edited by Baldwin and Anne O. Krueger. Chicago: University of Chicago Press.

———. 1985. *The Political Economy of U.S. Import Policy.* Cambridge, Mass.: The MIT Press.

Bayard, Thomas O., Joseph Pelzman, and Jorge Perez Lopez. 1983. Stakes and Risks in Economic Sanctions. *World Economy* 6:73–88.

Bendor, Jonathan, and Dilip Mookherjee. 1987. Institutional Structure and the Logic of Collective Action. *American Political Science Review* 81:129–54.

Bhagwati, Jagdish N. 1988. *Protectionism.* Cambridge, Mass.: MIT Press.

Bhagwati, Jagdish N., and T. N. Srinivasan. 1976. Optimal Trade Policy and Compensation under Endogenous Uncertainty: The Phenomenon of Market Disruption. *Journal of International Economics* 6:317–36.

Bidwell, R. L. 1970. *Currency Conversion Tables: A Hundred Years of Change.* London: Rex Collings.

Boadway, Robin, and David E. Wildasin. 1984. *Public Sector Economics,* 2d ed. Boston: Little, Brown.

Bourne, Kenneth, and D. Cameron Watt. 1987. *British Documents on Foreign Affairs: Reports and Papers from the Foreign Office Confidential Print,* Part I: *From the Mid-Nineteenth Century to the First World War,* Series F, *Europe,* Vol. 13, *France 1908–1913.* Frederick, Md.: University Publications of America.

Brada, Josef C. 1985. Review Article: Soviet Subsidization of Eastern Europe: The Primacy of Economics over Politics? *Journal of Comparative Economics* 9:80–92.

130

Brada, Josef C., and Jose A. Mendez. 1983. Regional Economic Integration and the Volume of Intra-Regional Trade: A Comparison of Developed and Developing Country Experience. *Kyklos* 36:589–603.

Brander, James, and Barbara Spencer. 1984. Export Subsidies and International Market Share Rivalry. *Journal of International Economics* 18:82–100.

Bueno de Mesquita, Bruce. 1980. Theories of International Conflict: An Analysis and an Appraisal. In *Handbook of Political Conflict: Theory and Research,* edited by Ted Robert Gurr. New York: Free Press.

———. 1981. *The War Trap.* New Haven, Conn.: Yale University Press.

Bueno de Mesquita, Bruce, and David Lalman. 1992. *War and Reason: Domestic and International Imperatives.* New Haven, Conn.: Yale University Press.

Bureau de la Statistique Generale. 1923. *Annuare Statistique de la France.* Paris: Ministere du Commerce de L'industry des Postes et des Telegraphs.

Cacciapuoti, Vincenzo. 1928. *Relazioni Commerciali tra L'Italia e la Russia, 1878–1927.* Napoli: N. Joveneji.

Capie, Forrest. 1983. *Depression and Protectionism: Britain Between the Two World Wars.* London: Allen & Unwin.

Caves, Richard E., and Ronald W. Jones. 1973. *World Trade and Payments: An Introduction.* Boston: Little, Brown.

Chalmin, Ph. G. 1984. The Important Trends in Sugar Diplomacy before 1914. In *Crisis and Change in the International Sugar Economy, 1860–1914,* edited by Bill Albert and Adrian Graves. Norwich, Eng.: ISC Press.

Chan, Kenneth S. 1985. The International Negotiating Game: Some Evidence from the Tokyo Round. *Review of Economics and Statistics* 67:456–64.

Christensen, Thomas J., and Jack Snyder. 1990. Chain Gangs and Passed Bucks: Predicting Alliance Patterns in Multipolarity. *International Organization* 44:137–68.

Clarke, Roger A., and Dubravko J. I. Matko. 1983. *Soviet Economic Facts, 1917–81.* 21st ed. New York: St. Martin's Press.

Cohen, Benjamin J. [1974] 1991. The Revolution in Atlantic Economic Relations: A Bargain Comes Unstuck. In *Crossing Frontiers: Explorations in International Political Economy,* edited by Cohen. Boulder, Colo.: Westview.

Conybeare, John A. C. 1983. Tariff Protection in Developed and Developing Countries. *International Organization* 37:441–68.

———. 1984. Public Goods, Prisoner's Dilemmas, and the International Political Economy. *International Studies Quarterly* 28:5–22.

———. 1987. *Trade Wars: The Theory and Practice of International Commercial Rivalry.* New York: Columbia University Press.

———. 1992. A Portfolio Diversification Model of Alliances: The Triple Alliance and the Triple Entente, 1879–1914. *Journal of Conflict Resolution* 36:52–85.

Corden, Max. 1986. The Normative Theory of International Trade. In *International Trade: Surveys of Theory and Policy: Selections from the Handbook*

131

of International Economics, edited by Ronald W. Jones. Amsterdam: North-Holland Press.

Deardorff, Alan V. 1984. Testing Trade Theories and Predicting Trade Flows. In *Handbook of International Economics,* edited by R. W. Jones and P. B. Kenen. Amsterdam: North-Holland Press.

Deardorff, Alan V., and Robert M. Stern. 1987. Current Issues in Trade Policy: An Overview. In *U.S. Trade Policies in a Changing World Economy,* edited by Stern. Cambridge, Mass.: MIT Press.

Department of Finance. 1905, 1920. *Annual Return of the Foreign Trade of the Empire of Japan.* Tokyo.

Dilks, David. 1981. Introduction. In *Retreat from Power: Studies in British Foreign Policy of the Twentieth Century,* Vol. I, *1906–1939,* edited by Dilks. London: Macmillan Press.

Dixit, Avinash. 1986. Trade Policy: An Agenda for Research. *In Strategic Trade Policy and the New International Economics,* edited by Paul R. Krugman. Cambridge, Mass.: MIT Press.

Dixit, Avinash. 1987. How Should the United States Respond to Other Countries' Trade Policies? In *U.S. Trade Policies in a Changing World Economy,* edited by Robert M. Stern. Cambridge, Mass.: MIT Press.

Downs, George W., and David M. Rocke. 1990. *Tacit Bargaining, Arms Races, and Arms Control.* Ann Arbor: University of Michigan Press.

Doyle, Michael W. 1986. Liberalism and World Politics. *American Political Science Review* 80:1,151–69.

Duncan, George T., and Randolph M. Siverson. 1982. Flexibility of Alliance Partner Choice in a Multipolar System: Models and Tests. *International Studies Quarterly* 26:511–38.

Eaton, Jonathan, and Gene M. Grossman. 1983. Optimal Trade and Industrial Policy under Oligopoly. National Bureau of Economic Research Working Paper No. 1236.

Ebeling, Hugo. 1914. *Wirtschaftliche Probleme bei dem deutsch-englischen Zuckerhandel.* Karlsruhe, Ger.: Hofbuchdruckerei und Verlag.

Eichengreen, Barry. 1986. The Political Economy of the Smoot-Hawley Tariff. National Bureau of Economic Research Working Paper No. 2001.

Ekelund, Robert B., and Robert D. Tollison. 1981. *Mercantilism as a Rent-Seeking Society: Economic Regulation in Historical Perspective.* College Station: Texas A & M Press.

Fearon, James. 1992. Threats to Use Force: Costly Signals and Bargaining in International Crises. Ph.D. diss., University of California, Berkeley.

Finlayson, Jock A., and Mark W. Zacher. 1981. The GATT and the Regulation of Trade Barriers: Regime Dynamics and Functions. *International Organization* 35:561–603.

Fitzpatrick, Gary L., and Marilyn J. Modlin. 1986. *Direct-Line Distances.* International ed. Metuchen, N.J.: Scarecrow Press.

132

Fox, John. 1991. *Regression Diagnostics.* Beverly Hills, Calif.: Sage.

Frank, Robert H. 1988. *Passions within Reason: The Strategic Role of the Emotions.* New York: W. W. Norton, 74–75.

Frankel, Jeffrey A. 1992. Is Japan Creating a Yen Bloc in East Asia and the Pacific? Paper presented at the National Bureau of Economic Research.

Frieden, Jeff. 1988. Sectoral Conflict and U.S. Foreign Economic Policy. *International Organization* 42:59–90.

Friedman, James W. 1983. *Oligopoly Theory.* New York: Cambridge University Press, 131.

———. 1977. *Oligopoly and the Theory of Games.* Amsterdam: North-Holland Press.

Fudenberg, D., and E. Maskin. 1986. The Folk Theorem in Repeated Games with Discounting and Incomplete Information. *Econometrica* 52:87–100.

Fudenberg, Drew, and Jean Tirole. 1991. *Game Theory.* Cambridge, Mass.: MIT Press.

Gallant, Ronald, and J. Jeffery Goebel. 1976. Nonlinear Regression with Autocorrelated Errors. *Journal of the American Statistical Association* 71:961–67.

Gasiorowski, Mark. 1986. Economic Interdependence and International Conflict: Some Cross-National Evidence. *International Studies Quarterly* 30:23–38.

Gasiorowski, Mark, and Solomon W. Polachek. 1982. Conflict and Interdependence: East-West Trade and Linkages in the Era of Detente. *Journal of Conflict Resolution* 26:709–29.

Gilpin, Robert G. 1975. *U.S. Power and the Multinational Corporation: The Political Economy of Direct Foreign Investment.* New York: Basic.

———. 1981. *War and Change in the International System.* Princeton, N.J.: Princeton University Press.

Gochman, Charles S., and Zeev Maoz. 1984. Militarized Interstate Disputes, 1816–1976: Procedures, Patterns, and Insights. *Journal of Conflict Resolution* 28:585–616.

Goldstein, Judith. Forthcoming. *Interests, Ideas, and American Foreign Economic Policy.* Ithaca, N.Y.: Cornell University Press.

Goldstein, Morris, and Mohsin S. Khan. 1984. Income and Price Effects in Foreign Trade. In *Handbook of International Economics,* edited by R. W. Jones and P. B. Kenen. Amsterdam: North-Holland Press.

Gooch, G. P., and Harold Temperley, editors. 1927–38. *British Documents on the Origins of the War, 1898–1914.* 11 vols. London: HM Stationery Office.

Gourevitch, Peter. 1986. *Politics in Hard Times: Comparative Responses to International Economic Crises.* Ithaca, N.Y.: Cornell University Press.

Gowa, Joanne. 1989. Bipolarity, Multipolarity, and Free Trade. *American Political Science Review* 83:1245–56.

Gregory, Paul R. 1982. *Russian National Income, 1885–1913.* New York: Cambridge University Press.

133

Grenville, J. A. S. 1974. *The Major International Treaties, 1914–1973.* London: Methuen.

Grieco, Joseph M. 1988. Anarchy and the Limits of Cooperation: A Realist Critique of the Newest Liberal Institutionalism. *International Organization* 42:485–508.

———. 1990. *Cooperation among Nations: Europe, America, and Non-tariff Barriers to Trade.* Ithaca, N.Y.: Cornell University Press.

Haggard, Stephan, and Beth A. Simmons. 1987. Theories of International Regimes. *International Organization* 41:491–517.

Hardach, Gerd. 1977. *The First World War, 1914–1918.* Berkeley: University of California Press.

Helpman, Elhanan. 1987. Comment on the National Defense Argument for Government Intervention in Trade. In *U.S. Trade Policies in a Changing World Economy,* edited by Robert M. Stern. Cambridge, Mass.: MIT Press.

Hibbs, Douglas A. 1974. Problems of Statistical Estimation and Causal Inference in Time-Series Regression Models. In *Sociological Methodology,* edited by Herbert L. Costner. San Francisco: Jossey-Bass.

Hillman, Ayre L. 1989. *The Political Economy of Protection.* New York: Harwood Academic Publishers.

Hirschman, Albert O. [1945] 1980. *National Power and the Structure of Foreign Trade.* Berkeley: University of California Press.

Holsti, Ole R., Terrence Hopmann, and John D. Sullivan. 1973. *Unity and Disintegration in International Alliances.* New York: John Wiley.

Howell, Llewellyn D. 1983. A Comparative Study of the WEIS and COPDAB Data Sets. *International Studies Quarterly* 27:149–59.

International Monetary Fund. 1950, 1956, 1966, 1976, 1986. *Direction of Trade.* Washington, D.C.: International Monetary Fund.

Irwin, Douglas A. 1988. Welfare Effects of British Free Trade: Debate and Evidence from the 1940s. *Journal of Political Economy* 96:1,142–64.

Jervis, Robert. 1985. From Balance to Concert: A Study of International Security Cooperation. *World Politics* 39:58–79.

———. 1988. Realism, Game Theory, and Cooperation. *World Politics* 60: 317–49.

Johnson, Harry G. 1953–54. Optimum Tariffs and Retaliation. *Review of Economic Studies* 21:142–53.

Kaempfer, William H., and Anton D. Lowenberg. 1992. *International Economic Sanctions: A Public Choice Perspective.* Boulder, Colo.: Westview Press.

Katzenstein, Peter J., editor. 1978. *Between Power and Plenty: Foreign Economic Policies of Advanced Industrialized States.* Madison: University of Wisconsin Press.

Kennedy, Paul. 1980. *The Rise of the Anglo-German Antagonism, 1860–1914.* London: Allen & Unwin.

———. 1985. The First World War and the International Power System. In

Military Strategy and the Origins of the First World War, edited by Steven E. Miller. Princeton, N.J.: Princeton University Press.

Keohane, Robert O. 1980. The Theory of Hegemonic Stability and Changes in International Economic Regimes, 1967–1977. In *Change in the International System*, edited by Ole R. Holsti, Randolph M. Siverson, and Alexander L. George. Boulder, Colo.: Westview.

———. 1984. *After Hegemony: Cooperation and Discord in the World Political Economy*. Princeton, N.J.: Princeton University Press.

———. 1988. Alliances, Threats, and the Uses of Neorealism. *International Security* 13:169–76.

Keohane, Robert O., and Joseph S. Nye. 1977. *Politics and Interdependence: World Politics in Transition*. Boston: Little, Brown.

Keohane, Robert O., and Joseph S. Nye, editors. 1970. *Transnational Relations and World Politics*. Cambridge, Mass.: Harvard University Press.

Kindleberger, Charles P. 1973. *The World in Depression, 1929–1939*. Berkeley: University of California Press.

———. 1986. Hierarchy versus Inertial Cooperation. *International Organization* 40:841–47.

Knorr, Klaus. 1977. International Economic Leverage and Its Uses. In *Economic Issues and National Security*, edited by Knorr and Frank N. Traeger. Lawrence, Kan.: Allen Press.

Krasner, Stephen D. 1976. State Power and the Structure of International Trade. *World Politics* 28:317–47.

Kreps, David M., Paul Milgrom, John Roberts, and Robert Wilson. 1982. Rational Cooperation in the Finitely Repeated Prisoners' Dilemm. *Journal of Economic Theory* 27:245–52.

Kreps, David M., and Robert Wilson. 1982. Reputation and Imperfect Information. *Journal of Economic Theory* 27:253–79.

Krugman, Paul R. 1986. Introduction: New Thinking about Trade Policy. In *Strategic Trade Policy and the New International Economics*, edited by Krugman. Cambridge, Mass.: MIT Press.

———. 1987. Strategic Sectors and International Competition. In *U.S. Trade Policies in a Changing World Economy*, edited by Robert M. Stern. Cambridge, Mass.: MIT Press.

Krugman, Paul R., and Maurice Obstfeld. 1988. *International Economics: Theory and Policy*. Glenview, Ill.: Scott, Foresman.

Lairson, Thomas D., and David Skidmore. 1993. *International Political Economy: The Struggle for Power and Wealth*. Fort Worth, Tex.: Harcourt Brace Jovanovich College Publishers.

Lake, David A. 1988. *Power, Protection, and Free Trade: International Sources of U.S. Commercial Strategy, 1887–1939*. Ithaca, N.Y.: Cornell University Press.

Lalman, David, and David Newman. 1991. Alliance Formation and National Security. *International Interactions* 16:239–53.

Laver, Michael. 1980. Political Solutions to the Collective Action Problem. *Political Studies* 28:195–209.

Lavergne, Real P. 1983. *The Political Economy of U.S. Tariffs: An Empirical Analysis.* Toronto, Can.: Academic.

League of Nations. 1926. *Memorandum on the Balance of Payments and Foreign Trade Balances, 1911–1925.* Vol. 1. Geneva: League of Nations.

———. 1933. *International Trade Statistics, 1931 and 1932.* Geneva: League of Nations.

Leamer, Edward E., and Robert M. Stern. 1970. *Quantitative International Economics.* Boston: Allyn & Bacon.

Lebow, Richard Ned. 1985. Conclusion. In *Psychology and Deterrence,* edited by Robert Jervis, Lebow, and Janice Gross Stein. Baltimore, Md.: Johns Hopkins University Press, 303–32.

Levy, Jack S. 1983. *War in the Modern Great Power System, 1495–1975.* Lexington: University Press of Kentucky.

Liesner, Thelma. Rev. ed. 1989. *One Hundred Years of Economic Statistics.* New York: The Economist.

Linneman, Hans. 1966. *An Econometric Study of International Trade Flows.* Amsterdam: North-Holland.

Lipson, Charles. 1991. Why Are Some International Agreements Informal? *International Organization* 45:495–538.

Liska, George. 1962. *Nations in Alliance: The Limits of Interdependence.* Baltimore, Md.: Johns Hopkins University Press.

Lohmann, Susanne, and Sharyn O'Halloran. 1991. Delegation Mechanisms in International Trade: Congress, the President, and U.S. Protectionism. Paper prepared for the annual meeting of the American Political Science Association. Washington, D.C.

Luce, R. Duncan, and Howard Raiffa. 1958. *Games and Decisions: Introduction and Critical Survey.* New York: John Wiley.

Maddala, G. S. 1988. *Introduction to Econometrics.* New York: Macmillan.

Magee, Stephen P., William A. Brock, and Leslie Young. 1989. *Black Hole Tariffs and Endogenous Policy Theory: Political Economy in General Equilibrium.* New York: Cambridge University Press.

Mansfield, Edward D. Forthcoming. *Power, Trade, and War.* Princeton, N.J.: Princeton University Press.

Marrese, Michael, and Jan Vanous. 1983. Unconventional Gains from Trade. *Journal of Comparative Economics* 7:382–99.

Marshall, Alfred. 1926. *Official Papers of Alfred Marshall.* London: Macmillan.

Martin, Lisa L. 1992. *Coercive Cooperation: Explaining Multilateral Economic Sanctions.* Princeton, N.J.: Princeton University Press.

Mastanduno, Michael. 1988. The Management of Alliance Export Control Policy: American Leadership and the Politics of COCOM. In *Controlling East-West Trade: Power, Politics, and Policies,* edited by Gary K. Bertsch.

McClelland, Charles D. 1983. Let the User Beware. *International Studies Quarterly* 27:169–77.

McCloskey, Donald N. 1980. Margnanimous Albion: Free Trade and British National Income, 1841–1881. *Explorations in Economic History* 17:303–20.

McKeown, Timothy James. 1982. The Rise and Decline of the Open Trading Regime of the Nineteenth Century. Ph.D. diss. Stanford University.

———. 1983. Hegemonic Stability Theory and Nineteenth Century Tariff Levels in Europe. *International Organization* 38:73–91.

———. 1984. Firms and Tariff Regime Change: Explaining the Demand for Protection. *World Politics* 36:214–33.

———. 1991. A Liberal Trade Order? The Long-Run Pattern of Imports to the Advanced Capitalist States. *International Studies Quarterly* 35:151–72.

McMillan, John. 1986. *Game Theory in International Economics.* New York: Harwood Academic Publishers.

Milgrom, Paul, and John Roberts. 1982. Limit Pricing and Entry under Incomplete Information: An Equilibrium Analysis. *Econometrica* 50:443–59.

Milward, Alan S. 1981. Tariffs as Constitutions. In *The International Politics of Surplus Capacity,* edited by S. Strange and R. Tooze. London: Allen & Unwin.

———. 1979. *War, Economy, and Society, 1939–1945.* Berkeley: University of California Press.

Mitchell, Brian R. 1980. *European Historical Statistics, 1750–1975.* London: Butler & Tanner.

———. 1982. *International Historical Statistics: Africa and Asia.* New York: New York University Press.

———. 1983. *International Historical Statistics: The Americas and Australia.* Detroit: Gale Research.

Monger, George. 1963. *The End of Isolation: British Foreign Policy, 1900–1907.* London: Thomas Nelson.

Morgenthau, Hans. [1948] 1973. *Politics among Nations.* New York: Knopf.

Morrow, James D. 1991. Alliances and Asymmetry: An Alternative Aggregation Model of Alliances. *American Journal of Political Science* 35:904–33.

Nelson, Douglas. 1988. Endogenous Tariff Theory: A Critical Survey. *American Journal of Political Science* 32:796–837.

Niou, Emerson M. S., Peter C. Ordeshook, and Gregory F. Rose. 1989. *The Balance of Power: Stability in International Systems.* Cambridge, Eng.: Cambridge University Press.

Nye, John Vincent. 1991. The Myth of Free-Trade Britain and Fortress France: Tariffs and Trade in the Nineteenth Century. *Journal of Economic History* 51:23–46.

O'Brien, Patrick K., and Geoffrey Allen Pignam. 1992. Free Trade, British Hegemony, and the International Economic Order in the Nineteenth Century. *Review of International Studies* 18:89–113.

137

Offer, Avner. 1989. *The First World War: An Agrarian Interpretation*. New York: Oxford University Press.

Olson, Mancur. [1965] 1971. *The Logic of Collective Action: Public Goods and the Theory of Groups*. Cambridge, Mass.: Harvard University Press.

Organski, A. F. K., and Jacek Kugler. 1980. *The War Ledger*. Chicago: University of Chicago Press.

Oye, Kenneth A. 1992. *Economic Discrimination and Political Exchange: World Political Economy in the 1930s and 1980s*. Princeton, N.J.: Princeton University Press.

———. 1985a. Explaining Cooperation under Anarchy: Strategies and Institutions. *World Politics* 38:1–24.

———. 1985b. The Sterling-Dollar-Franc Triangle: Monetary Diplomacy, 1929–1937. *World Politics* 38:173–99.

———. 1979. The Domain of Choice: International Constraints and the Carter Administration. In *Eagle Entangled: U.S. Foreign Policy in a Complex World*, edited by Oye, Donald Rothschild, and Robert J. Lieber. New York: Longman.

Pahre, Robert. 1990. A General Model of Economic and Security Cooperation and the Case of Postwar Europe. Typescript, University of Rochester.

Pelzman, Joseph. 1977. Trade Creation and Trade Diversion in the Council of Mutual Economic Assistance, 1954–1970. *American Economic Review* 67:713–22.

Pincus, Jonathan J. 1977. *Pressure Groups and Politics in Antebellum Tariffs*. New York: Columbia University Press.

Polachek, Solomon William. 1978. Dyadic Disputes: An Economic Perspective. *Papers, Peace Science Society (International)* 28:67–80.

———. 1980. Conflict and Trade. *Journal of Conflict Resolution* 24:55–78.

Pollins, Brian M. 1989a. Does Trade Still Follow the Flag? *American Political Science Review* 83:465–80.

———. 1989b. Conflict, Cooperation, and Commerce: The Effects of International Political Interactions on Bilateral Trade Flows. *American Journal of Political Science* 33:737–61.

Posen, Barry R. 1984. *The Sources of Military Doctrine: France, Britain, and Germany between the World Wars*. Ithaca, N.Y.: Cornell University Press.

Powell, Robert. 1991. The Problem of Absolute and Relative Gains in International Relations. *American Political Science Review* 85:1,303–20.

———. 1992. Bargaining in the Shadow of Power. Typescript.

Rasmusen, Eric. 1989. *Games and Information: An Introduction to Game Theory*. New York: Basil Blackwell.

Ray, Edward John. 1981. The Determinants of Tariff and Nontariff Trade Restrictions in the United States. *Journal of Political Economy* 89:105–21.

Richardson, J. David. 1987. Comment on "How Should the United States Respond to Other Countries' Trade Policies?" In *U.S. Trade Policies in a Changing World Economy*, edited by Robert M. Stern. Cambridge, Mass.: MIT Press.

———. 1990. The Political Economy of Strategic Trade Policy. *International Organization* 44:107–35.

Rogowski, Ronald. 1989. *Commerce and Coalitions.* Princeton, N.J.: Princeton University Press.

Root, William A. 1984. Trade Controls That Work. *Foreign Policy* 56:61–80.

Rosecrance, Richard, editor. 1976. *America as an Ordinary Country: U.S. Foreign Policy and the Future.* Ithaca, N.Y.: Cornell University Press.

Ruggie, John Gerard. 1972. Collective Goods and Future International Collaboration. *American Political Science Review* 66:874–93.

———. 1982. International Regimes, Transactions, and Change: Embedded Liberalism in the Postwar Economic Order. *International Organization* 36:379–415.

Russett, Bruce M. 1971. An Empirical Typology of International Military Alliances. *Midwest Journal of Political Science* 15:262–89.

———. 1985. The Mysterious Case of Vanishing Hegemony. *International Organization* 39:207–32.

Russett, Bruce, and Harvey Starr. 1992. *World Politics: The Menu for Choice.* New York: W. H. Freeman.

Salisbury, Lord Robert. 1870. The Terms of Peace. *Quarterly Review* 129:540–56.

Schroeder, Paul W. 1976. Alliances, 1815–1945: Weapons of Power and Tools of Management. In *Historical Dimensions of National Security Problems,* edited by Klaus Knorr. Lawrence: University of Kansas Press.

Sebenius, James K. 1983. Negotiation Arithmetic: Adding and Subtracting Issues and Parties. *International Organization* 37:281–316.

Shapiro, Carl. 1989. Theories of Oligopoly Behavior. In *Handbook of Industrial Organization,* Vol. 1, edited by Richard Schmalensee and Robert D. Willig. Amsterdam: North-Holland Press.

Siverson, Randolph M., and Juliann Emmons. 1991. Birds of a Feather: Democratic Political Systems and Alliance Choices in the Twentieth Century. *Journal of Conflict Resolution* 35:285–306.

Siverson, Randolph M., and Joel King. 1980. Attributes of Alliance Membership and War Participation, 1815–1965. *American Journal of Political Science* 24:1–15.

Small, Melvin,, and J. David Singer. 1969. Formal Alliances, 1816–1965: An Extension of the Basic Data. *Journal of Peace Research* 3:257–82.

———. 1982. *Resort to Arms: International and Civil Wars, 1816–1980.* Beverly Hills, Calif.: Sage.

Snidal, Duncan. 1985a. Coordination versus Prisoners' Dilemma: Implications for International Cooperation and Regimes. *American Political Science Review* 79:923–42.

———. 1985b. The Limitations of Hegemonic Stability Theory. *International Organization* 39:579–614.

———. 1991. Relative Gains and the Pattern of International Cooperation. *American Political Science Review* 85:701–26.

Snyder, Glenn H., and Paul Diesing. 1977. *Conflict among Nations: Bargaining, Decision Making, and System Structure in International Crisis.* Princeton, N.J.: Princeton University Press.

Snyder, Glenn H. 1984. The Security Dilemma in Alliance Politics. *World Politics* 36:461–95.

———. 1990. Alliance Theory: A Neorealist First Cut. *Journal of International Affairs* 103–23.

———. 1991. Alliances, Balance, and Stability. *International Organization* 45:121–42.

Snyder, Jack. 1984. *The Ideology of the Offensive: Military Decision Making and the Disasters of 1914.* Ithaca, N.Y.: Cornell University Press.

Srinivasan, T. N. 1987. The National Defense Argument for Government Intervention in Foreign Trade. In *U.S. Trade Policies in a Changing World Economy,* edited by Robert M. Stern. Cambridge, Mass.: MIT Press.

Stein, Arthur A. 1984. The Hegemon's Dilemma: Great Britain, the United States, and the International Economic Order. *International Organization* 38:355–86.

———. 1990. *Why Nations Cooperate: Circumstance and Choice in International Relations.* Ithaca, N.Y.: Cornell University Press.

Steiner, Z. S. 1977. *Britain and the Origins of the First World War.* London: Macmillan.

Stigler, George J. 1964. A Theory of Oligopoly. *Journal of Political Economy* 72:44–61.

Taylor, Michael. 1976. *Anarchy and Cooperation.* London: John Wiley.

———. 1987. *The Possibility of Cooperation.* Cambridge, Eng.: Cambridge University Press.

Telser, L. G. 1980. A Theory of Self-Enforcing Agreements. *Journal of Business* 53:27–44.

Tinbergen, Jan. 1962. *Shaping the World Economy: Suggestions for an International Economic Policy.* New York: Twentieth Century Fund.

Tirole, Jean. 1988. *Industrial Organization.* Cambridge, Mass.: MIT Press.

Tollison, Robert D., and Thomas D. Willett. 1979. An Economic Theory of Mutually Advantageous Issue Linkages. *International Organization* 33:425–49.

Trachtenberg, Marc. 1991. *History and Strategy.* Princeton, N.J.: Princeton University Press.

United States Census Bureau. 1915. *Statistical Abstracts of the United States.* Washington, D.C.: U.S. Government Printing Office.

United States Department of Commerce and Labor Bureau of Statistics. 1914, 1921, and 1931. *Foreign Commerce and Navigation of the United States.* Washington, D.C.: U.S. Government Printing Office.

United States Hydrographic Office. 1912, 1936. *Table of Distances in Nautical and Statute Miles.* Washington, D.C.: United States Hydrographic Office.

———. 1965, 1989. *Distance between Ports.* Washington, D.C.: United States Hydrographic Office.

United States Treasury Department. 1904, 1905, 1912, 1913, 1919, 1920. *Circulars.* Washington, D.C.: U.S. Government Printing Office.

Van Evera, Stephen. 1984. The Cult of the Offensive and the Origins of the First World War. *International Security* 9:58–107.

Viner, Jacob. 1948. Power vs. Plenty as Objectives of Foreign Policy in the Seventeenth and Eighteenth Centuries. *World Politics* 1:1–29.

von Haberler, Gottfried. 1933. *The Theory of International Trade with Its Applications to Commercial Policy.* London: William Hodge.

Walt, Stephen M. 1987. *The Origins of Alliances.* Ithaca, N.Y.: Cornell University Press.

———. 1989. Alliances in Theory and Practice: What Lies Ahead? *Journal of International Affairs* 43:1.

Waltz, Kenneth N. 1979. *Theory of International Politics.* Reading, Mass.: Addison-Wesley.

Weingast, Barry R., and William Marshall. 1988. The Industrial Organization of Congress. *Journal of Political Economy* 96:132–63.

White, Halbert. 1980. A Heteroskedasticity-Consistent Covariance Matrix Estimator and a Direct Test for Heteroskedasticity. *Econometrica* 48:817–38.

Willett, Thomas D., and Mehrdad Jalalighajar. 1983–84. U.S. Trade Policy and National Security. *Cato Journal* 3:717–27.

Williamson, Oliver. 1975. *Markets and Hierarchies: Analysis and Antitrust Implications, A Study in the Economics of Internal Organization.* New York: Free Press.

Wilson, Keith M. 1985. *The Policy of the Entente: Essays on the Determinants of British Foreign Policy.* Cambridge, Eng.: Cambridge University Press.

———. 1987. *Empire and Continent: Studies in British Foreign Policy from the 1880s to the First World War.* London: Mansell.

Winham, Gilbert R. 1986. *International Trade and the Tokyo Round Negotiation.* Princeton, N.J.: Princeton University Press.

Wonnacott, Paul. 1987. The United States and Canada: The Quest for Free Trade. *Policy Analyses in International Economics No. 16.* Washington, D.C.: Institute for International Economics.

Yarbrough, Beth, and Robert M. Yarbrough. 1986. Reciprocity, Bilateralism, and Economic Hostages: Self-Enforcing Agreements in International Trade. *International Studies Quarterly* 30:7–22.

———. 1987. Cooperation in the Liberalization of International Trade: After Hegemony, What? *International Organization* 41:1–26.

———. 1991. *The World Economy: Trade and Finance.* 2d ed. Hinsdale, Ill.: Dryden Press.

————. 1992. *Cooperation and Governance in International Trade: The Strategic Organizational Approach.* Princeton, N.J.: Princeton University Press.

Yeager, Leland B., and David G. Tureck. 1983–84. Realism and Free-Trade Policy. *Cato Journal* 3:645–66.

Young, Oran R. 1975. "Introduction." In *Bargaining: Formal Theories of Negotiation,* edited by Young. Urbana: University of Illinois Press.

Index